RIGHT BEFORE OUR EYES:

Latinos Past, Present & Future

By Robert Montemayor
with Henry Mendoza

SCHOLARGY

CUSTOM PUBLISHING

RIGHT BEFORE OUR EYES:
Latinos Past, Present & Future

By Robert Montemayor
with Henry Mendoza

ID# 3094
ISBN: 1-59247-656-2

Printed in The United States of America

Copyright © 2004 by The Tomás Rivera Policy Institute

Published and Distributed by Scholargy Publishing, Inc.

Scholargy Publishing
1555 W. University Drive, Suite 108
Tempe, AZ 85281
www.scholargy.com

This book is dedicated to

Augustine and Maria Montemayor

and

Henry and Esther Mendoza

RIGHT BEFORE OUR EYES:
Latinos Past, Present & Future

TABLE OF CONTENTS

Foreword

By Sol Trujillo

This book is about a huge and uniquely American opportunity that is waiting to be unlocked and which can benefit people in all walks of life – business, education, politics, public service and dozens of other parts of our lives here in the United States. That opportunity is to tap into the now robust and powerful and growing Latino population in this country.

Most Americans haven't recognized the dynamism of the Latino market. But the fact is that Latinos are growing exponentially in the United States – faster than any other element of American society. Another fact is that Latinos reflect a positive attitude toward all that is special to America – the work ethic, integrity, diligence, scholarship and more.

At this point virtually no one has stepped forward to unlock the talent and creativity of the Latino population base. Those who figure out how to capitalize on that talent and creativity will make a positive difference in their companies, their communities, their political structures and more. More important, they will make a positive difference for themselves and for this nation which needs to leverage every opportunity today to be competitive on the world stage. This book provides hard facts and data that will serve individuals who want to stay ahead of the curve and create a competitive advantage for themselves and for those around them.

The idea for this book has been percolating in my mind since the early 1980's. As I was "climbing the ladder" in the business world over the past 30 years, I became increasingly disappointed and concerned that Hispanics were not advancing to the top decision making positions in our society. Very few Hispanics were making significant progress toward the upper levels of the policy making positions in institutions such as corporations, government, media, education, the judiciary and the military.

Yet, even in the early 1980s, and then the 1990s, political pundits and national publications were heralding "The Decade of the Hispanic" or "The

Year of the Hispanic". However, when you looked at our statistical profile – the number of Hispanics that were on Fortune 1000 boards of directors, CEOs, United States senators, governors, Supreme Court justices, school district superintendents, university presidents, generals and admirals in the military, etc. the numbers just were not there. Hispanics were missing in action.

At the same time, Latinos' contributions in making the United States the undisputed political, military and economic leader among nations have been nothing short of stellar.

Almost 450 years ago, Spanish explorer Pedro Menéndez de Avilés established the first permanent European settlement in the New World in St. Augustine, Florida. This was 40 years before the British arrived at Jamestown.

Latinos have fought and died for this country in every war, earning 42 Medals of Honor and countless other distinctions for courage.

When this nation's infrastructure was being built, Hispanics were there. The sweat and sometimes the lives of Hispanic workers are woven into the foundations and building blocks of the nation's railroads, highways, utilities, dams, mines, homes and skyscrapers. Much of the agricultural success of this country is due to the Mexican migrant workers and their families toiling in the fields in extreme conditions.

In business, science, education, medicine, the fine arts, literature, government, the entertainment industry and the sports world, Latinos have left their indelible mark as they helped make this country a better place in which to live. Their influences are ubiquitous, including the names we give to many of our cities and streets, the architecture of our homes, the food we eat, and the many Spanish words that have infiltrated the English language and are part of our daily lexicon.

Yet, despite their substantial contributions to this great country we live in, Latinos continue to be virtually excluded within institutional power structures. While Latinos represent about 14 percent of this nation's population, they are woefully underrepresented in the top echelons of institutions. For example, there are more than 10,000 board of director seats among the Fortune 1000 companies, yet only slightly more than 200 are occupied by Latinos. It would take more than seven times that number just to reflect the marketplace.

At the same time, the attractiveness of the Hispanic marketplace in this country has grown faster than expectations, representing a huge opportunity for businesses that have the astute insights to capitalize on the phenomenon. In 2004, the United States' estimated 40 million Hispanics are spending nearly $700 billion on goods and services. If this country's Latinos were a nation, their gross domestic product (GDP) would rank ninth in the world, just below Canada. Even more astounding is the projected growth rate for this economic colossus. By 2008, researchers are predicting that Hispanics' buying power will be about $1 trillion per year, which would represent an astounding growth rate of over 450 percent since 1990 when Hispanic purchasing totaled $222 billion. Corporate America cannot afford to ignore this economic tsunami.

It is also important to note the country's labor force will be very dependent on Hispanics. It is projected that by 2020, one out of every six workers in the U.S. will be Hispanic. By 2050, it will be one out of every four. Remember, it is workers who pay into our social security and other support systems of our country. Further, it is projected that U.S. Hispanics, in this same time frame, will comprise about 25 percent of the U.S. population, marking an era in America when no group can claim to be the majority.

I am a person who is very proud of both my country and my heritage. At the same time, I am a free market capitalist. But as I have observed over time this disconnect between the the importance of Latinos in this country and then being excluded from the decision-making processes and structures that govern us, I believe it is time for the "bridging of this gap". Education, information, debate, dialogue and action have always been the most effective ways to create progress – those attributes are the hallmarks of our great democracy.

Now more than ever, it is time for change. This country cannot afford to remain "exclusionary" and "exclusive," particularly as it relates to the most dynamic segment of our country's population.

Having run large multi-billion dollar corporations in the U.S. and abroad, I have found that engaging all – rather than just some – employees leads to greater productivity and results. If only some can aspire to greater heights while others cannot, it becomes limiting and divisive. Whether this exclusionary approach toward Hispanics has happened consciously or not, it is time to put it behind us and welcome this important group into our country's top decision making hierarchies.

It is also evident that the Hispanic youth of our country also need role models to help them understand that when they work and get results, they can realistically achieve any position in this country's institutions – just like everyone else.

This environment can be very inspirational to achieve more, give more and collaborate more. It is extremely difficult today for Hispanic youth to appreciate what is attainable, given the lack of Hispanic role models in the media and other top leadership positions in this country's public and private sectors. We now have the opportunity to change this situation through understanding, education, removal of discriminatory barriers and "inclusive" strategies which will enable a full field of competitors.

Not long ago, when asked by a CEO who wanted to learn more about the Latino community what book he should read to gain insights that could help him, I began a search to identify the right book. I went to a leading book store in Southern California to find one which would meet the criteria. I was enthusiastic about this mission, assuming that since I was in Southern California this would not be a problem.

Upon entering the bookstore I went to the ethnic studies section and was dumbfounded. There was a full section of books related to the African American experiences. There were two bookshelves of both Asian American and Native American and *only six* books regarding Latinos! As I thumbed through a number of these, I noticed that the books each had its own unique focus on a point in history or topic.

This experience convinced me and my wife Corine to decide to initiate or sponsor the authoring of this book. It is obvious to us that there is a need for the authoring of several bodies of work that can be made available to our junior high, high school and collegiate students...or for the businesses of this country that need further understanding of this great unfolding market opportunity…or for the public policy makers who need to better understand the people they represent in setting policies which are important today and in the future.

This book was managed and administered under the leadership of Dr. Harry Pachon, President of The Tomás Rivera Policy Institute (TRPI) and Dr. Loui Olivas, Assistant Vice President for Academic Affairs and Professor, W. P. Carey School of Business, Arizona State University. Dr. Olivas and Dr. Pachon have done tremendous work bringing this to fruition, working with our authors, publisher and a whole series of other individuals. I thank them for their dedication to this book. It is important to note that all proceeds from this book will go to TRPI for further studies and additional book authorings.

I would also like to thank Henry Mendoza, one of the authors contributing to the book's completion. He has great passion for the subject given his many experiences in his personal life. Finally, I want to thank Robert Montemayor who did the majority of the research and work on the book. He also has lived the experience described in the book but even more importantly he has created a composite of several topic areas we should all strive to understand better. His passionate dedication and uncompromising approach enabled the beginning of a necessary dialogue and understanding for all. Without question the call to action in the closing chapter is the most important piece he puts forward — as someone once said "words without actions mean nothing."

Author's Note

We're often told that it is more about the journey than it is about the destination. And maybe it has been so with the writing of this book. The journey has been arduous if for no other reason than the writing was done in a mere six months — nothing short of a massive sprint.

The journey has taxed us and forced us to re-examine ourselves, not only as Latinos but as Americans. And we've arrived at the same conclusion, that we are one and the same – Latinos who are Americans and Americans who are Latinos. We are proud to be both and we are proud to live in a country where we can enjoy the benefits of both, presumably without restrictions, fear or trepidation.

When we started this project, we thought we knew our Latino culture. Between us we have more than 60 years of experience in journalism, business, public relations, and marketing, much of it within the Hispanic community. In retrospect, we only *thought* we knew our community. We confirmed what we thought we knew, but rejoiced in the fact that there is so much potential, so much that can be accomplished and so much that is within everyone's reach.

People like to have a sense of hope. They like to think there's a bright future. Whether you are 14 or 34 or 54, as Americans we like to believe that we can live out our dreams. Some may believe that's too much corn or too much B.S. given the vagaries of our world these days. The fact is that we both grew up with those kinds of dreams with amazingly similar experiences in places like Colton, California and Tahoka, Texas – entirely different parts of the country that turn out to be so different and yet so similar. And that similarity comes from our Latino roots.

Our parents dealt with many more obstacles than we did. They grew up with the racial name calling, the segregated schools, churches, restaurants and theaters, many of the same obstacles that we outline in this book. Yet, they persevered. They held the course.

They constantly pushed us. And they reminded us that, while America was a wonderful place to live, it also had its gauntlet of challenges, particularly for a couple of Mexican Americans like us.

As kids, we thought how difficult will it be? Things won't always be so racially oriented, or discriminatory or unfair. Many years later we learned the universal lesson – who said life was fair?

We both pursued careers in journalism because we thought we could right the wrongs. We thought we would write about injustices and educate people to make them go away. We thought we could effect needed changes in society. We thought we could make a difference. Sometimes we did. Most of the time we didn't.

There are some Latinos who may read this book and say, "So what? There's nothing new here." And for many – the *veteranos* of our community — that may be the case. But for a great many, who don't traffic on a daily basis with the issues that confront Hispanics, so much of what is in this book is new and is worth reading and is worth fully understanding.

Not everyone has a firm understanding of the Hispanic communities of America – not even Hispanics themselves. With few exceptions, the sons and daughters of our friends, to name a few, have no context of what it is to be a Hispanic in America. They have little connection with our rich, storied past, no sense of context in terms of the sacrifices that were made so they would not have to suffer the indignities that many – and that includes us – have had to suffer to scratch out a living in this country. They need to know the stories so they need to read the stories. This book is as much for them as anyone.

We also would implore those Latinos who are in midst of budding careers, or who are just starting families to take a more active approach to how they live their lives in this country. Take nothing for granted. Leave nothing to chance. Ask questions when you are not promoted. Ask questions when your child is not bringing home good grades. If you don't ask, you don't receive. And as we like to say, what's the worst anyone can say in asking questions? It is your right to ask, even when you are not satisfied with the first answer, or even second answer. This book is as much for you as anyone because it's your careers or your children's careers that could be on the line in the near future.

And to those who may say, "So what? There's nothing new here." We say, "Hey, chill out." Both of us have been exactly where you've been. Yeah, it's hard to keep the embers of activism burning over 20, 30 or 40 years. It's hard to read anything that we haven't already read, said or written before. All this falls into the category of been-there, done-that, thought-that.

With all due respect to all you *veteranos/veteranas,* we recognize that many out there have logged your time organizing, politicking, raising money for good causes, recognizing terrific role models, *being* terrific role models and pushing for the very goals that we advocate in this book. Many of you may feel that you've spent a lifetime pounding away at rock-hard issues that have made you weary, perhaps a bit jaded. We would say just two words to you, *y que* (so what)?

Again, no disrespect — we would ask you to set aside your cynicism. The issues that we rallied around 20, 30, or 40 years ago continue to stare at us: exclusion from leadership posts within the public and private sectors, continued challenges in education, abject poverty, equal rights that are not so equal, homeownership barriers borne of discrimination, a glaring lack of health care, and the list goes on. We're not telling you anything you don't already know. We would only tell you that the war over these issues is not over. There might not be anything new for you in this book, but your participation is still valuable. Your experience is needed. Your leadership and places as role models are needed by the hopeful generations of Hispanics that follow behind you. Regardless, you need to read this book just to catch up with the numbers.

So it has been about the journey, and we would be remiss if we didn't thank a few people who have made the trek more plausible:

First, we'd like to thank our wives, Virginia Lujano and Kris Mendoza, for their patience, support, input and love. For all the long hours, all the pots of coffee, all the encouragement, all the prodding, all the editing and readings, all the frank critiques, all the smiles when we most needed a smile – thank you.

We'd also like to give huge thanks Sol and Corine Trujillo, who commissioned this project and who have shown great courage and an undying fire in dealing with mammoth issues. Sol and Corine gave birth to this project when, one day while shopping at a local bookstore, they were appalled at the lack of books dealing with Hispanics. Why are we so marginalized, Sol and Corine wondered? Why so little literature about a culture with more than 500 years of history in the Western Hemisphere? The more they thought about it, the more they burned over the issue.

Sol and Corine Trujillo set out with a conception to do a mass media book on Hispanics, a literary work that would pack the latest information on Hispanics with a bit of editorial moxy and edge and, most important, a proposed set of recommendations. To his credit, Sol left us to our own devices to write the book as we thought it should be written. To be sure, he prodded and coached wherever he could. But he always left the manuscript in our hands. For that, we are most grateful.

At one time, Sol was chairman, president and CEO of US West and, most recently, he was CEO of Orange SA, one of the largest telecommunications companies in Europe. He understands corporate America. He knows how to navigate the political waters of both national parties. Quite simply, he knows how to play the game. This book is his vision as much as anyone's. It is his spirit upon that gave flight to this project.

We'd like to thank the entire staff at The Tomás Rivera Policy Institute, including Harry Pachon, Kathryn Grady, Andrea Gutierrez, Stephanie Lomibao and Robert Esqueda, for all their support and guidance.

A special round of thanks goes to our man at Arizona State University, Loui Olivas, who kept us on schedule and kept us laughing all through the project. Tireless, punctual, absorbed with the details and all the while maintaining a sense of levity – you can't ask for much more. As Assistant Vice President for Academic Affairs and Professor, W.P. Carey School of Business, ASU is extremely lucky to have him. And we give another strong round of thanks to Reid Boates, our literary agent/editor who became an honorary Hispanic during the project. Always upbeat, always positive, Reid urged us on every step of the way. His emails always ended with his signature, "Onward."

We not only give strong thanks to our parents but we also would like to dedicate our work to them. Without their undying love and support, we might not have made it this far. They were unflinching in their demands of us. The lessons were often tough, but it was about tough love from parents who never heard of the term. At the end of the day, they taught us well.

To Augustine and Maria Montemayor and Henry and Esther Mendoza, we dedicate this book to you.

Every good story usually has a bit of irony. This book project is no different. The project actually started with a telephone call from the late *Los Angeles Times* columnist and our close friend Frank Del Olmo in September of 2003. Frank had called to say that he had received a call from Harry Pachon, president of The Tomás Rivera Policy Institute, who had asked him to consider writing a book on the impact of Hispanics on America. Frank had passed on the book because he wanted to concentrate on the 2004 elections. Instead, Frank recommended to Pachon that we do the book. Frank then called both of us to give us the heads up.

I remember asking Frank, "So, what do you think?" Del Olmo's response: "Robert, it shouldn't be that hard. It's nothing that you guys don't already know. You'll be fine. It should be fun." Frank had a special way of understating things. As usual, no work worth doing is ever that easy. But we do owe a good bit of gratitude to Frank for his decision.

As it turned out, Frank del Olmo passed away in February while working at the *Los Angeles Times*. As a result of his untimely death, Frank's wife Magdalena del Olmo convinced the *Times* to publish a book of Frank's best editorials.

The irony? *Right Before Our Eyes* and Frank's book, *Frank del Olmo Commentaries on His Times* will both be released in September. None of us three had ever written a book. We're sure Frank would say he planned it that way.

RIGHT BEFORE OUR EYES:

Latinos Past, Present & Future

CHAPTER ONE

Right Before Our Eyes

- *Latinos are the largest and the youngest ethnic minority in the United States.*

- *At approximately 40 million today, Hispanics account for 13.7 percent of the U.S. population.*

- *By 2050, one of every four Americans will be Hispanic, a number that will exceed 100 million.*

- *In 2020, one out of six workers in the U.S. will be Latino; in 2050, it will be one out of every four.*

- *Hispanics will spend $700 billion this year, or a rate of $1.33 million per minute.*

- *In 2025, U.S. Hispanic consumer spending power will surpass $3 trillion, which would rank them as the world's fourth largest economy behind the U.S., Japan, and China.*

- *Hispanics possess 6 to 8 million votes poised for the 2004 presidential election; they are expected to represent the critical swing vote in six states.*

All of this has the ring of power, the kind of power that sparks market trends, affects the economy, and has politicians pandering for votes. This power is an illusion. Given these numbers, Latinos should be in the executive's seat of private corporations, in the judge's chair in courtrooms, in the legislator's seat at the local, state, or federal level. With this kind of power, we should be welcomed into the American mainstream of thought and policy. But we are not.

Maybe it's because too many citizens of the U.S. don't understand Latinos. We are one of this country's great contradictions. We are at once one of this continent's oldest inhabitants, arriving here more than five centuries ago, and its newest citizens, taking our first steps into America only a few minutes ago.

Latinos have provided the sweat for this nation's economy for most of a century, and have been the foot soldiers of its military for more than 200 years. We've been the grape-apple-figs-tomato-orange-almond-avocado-lettuce-onion-artichoke-grapefruit-apricot-cherry-pickers who made agriculture one of the nation's leading industries.

We've made careers of entry-level jobs and, in exceptional cases, managed to be awarded a Nobel Prize, and earned several dozen Medals of Honor.

We have roots in Mexico, Puerto Rico, Cuba, Spain, the Dominican Republic, Guatemala, Colombia, Honduras, Peru, Chile, Ecuador, El Salvador, Nicaragua or any number of other exotic places in Latin America. We left lands we love for a great nation we want to love.

We have been a quiet, respectful people – patient and dutifully civil. We have been taught not to expect too much – that God will provide. In that regard, we are as much a part of the Catholic Church as the Catholic Church is a part of us.

We live in the belief that our day will come, without ever defining when, let alone what exactly that day will bring. While we organize in pockets around the country, we do not organize as one and only rarely flex our collective political muscle. Mexican Americans have their political ambitions. As do Cuban Americans. And Puerto Ricans. And so on. For the time being, the parts are greater than the whole.

This may explain, in part, why this wonderfully rich, colorful, diverse, multicultural community does not reside in the halls of power. Why there is no meaningful representation of Hispanics at the highest levels of business, education, law, politics, or policy.

How did this happen? How did it happen that Latinos played such a significant role in this country's evolution, sharing its freedom, laboring in its fields, gathering around its dinner tables, and building the nation's infrastructure, and yet find ourselves excluded from the upper echelons of American power and decision-making?

More than 40 million Hispanics now reside all across the United States, from Washington to Florida, from Maine to California. Large metropolitan enclaves of Hispanics numbering in the millions are in New York, Miami, Chicago, Dallas, San Antonio, and Los Angeles.

Yet this only begs the resolution of key issues of leadership, exclusion from both public and private sector executive-level posts, untapped political capital, the need to cure education ills, health care, and dreadful poverty – all of which exist against the backdrop of an emerging middle class that is beginning to flex its economic muscle and demand its rightful place in American society. The question some have asked is this: "How much will Hispanics change America, and how much will America change them?"

What's in a Name?

Hispanics didn't even have a label until the 1960s, when a report by the Civil Rights Commission detailed the failing educational condition of Mexican Americans. Although the report only covered five southwestern states, it prompted the federal government to task the U.S. Census Bureau with collecting information about a community that had previously been known only as the "foreign-born."

"The U.S. always adds categories as issues arise," said Leo Estrada, Ph.D., a noted demographer, statistician, and UCLA professor who has studied the census, its methodology and history.

In the 1930s, the census bureau gave Mexicans their own category. In later years, as a result of lawsuits demanding reclassification, Mexicans were listed as "white." The Civil Rights Act of 1964 addressed discrimination based on race and color, but it did not affect Hispanic groups because they were, after all, white.

In 1972 the census bureau hired a young Latino from New Mexico by the name of Fernando del Rio to come up with a list of potential terms and test them on the Latino population. Under consideration were "Spanish

American," "Hispano," "persons of Spanish origin," "Latin American," "Mexican American," "Mexican," "Hispanic," and "Latino." (The terms "Hispanic" and "Latino" are used interchangeably for the purposes of this book. The term "Anglo" refers to non-Hispanic whites.)

In 1976, Latino civil rights groups (National Council of La Raza, the League of United Latin American Citizens, and the Mexican American Legal Defense and Educational Fund), along with then-Congressman Edward R. Roybal, joined forces to get Public Law 94-311 passed by Congress. This law created an umbrella for "Americans of Spanish origin or descent" and required that this group's welfare and progress be monitored. Finally, in 1977, the Office of Management and Budget issued Directive 15: "Race and Ethnic Standards for Federal Statistics and Administrative Reporting." It ushered in the official use of the word "Hispanic," which was defined as "a person of Mexican, Puerto Rican, Cuban, Central or South American or other Spanish culture or origin, regardless of race."

"Once it was imposed, it was the perfect bureaucratic solution," Estrada said, "because it was the most innocuous term." It was popular with legislators because it conveniently lumped a diverse population into a single category. Initially, it was neither popular nor understood by the newly christened Hispanic community, according to Estrada. "We go in the field and nobody knows what Hispanic means. Until you ask them, 'Are you Mexican, Puerto Rican, Cuban?' Only then do they realize they're Hispanic."

Although "Hispanic" was the ideal moniker for bureaucratic use, its creation was supported by census polls in which Hispanics preferred the term over other labels. For many, the term "Latino" had activist overtones, but it was a softer tag to the more dissident label "Chicano," which often personified Latinos who were two or three notches politically left-of-center. By default, Latino became an informal secondary term used to describe Hispanics. In time, the term Latino gained its own level of bureaucratic acceptance, and gained even greater use throughout the Southwest and parts of the East. Today, however, polls show a stronger preference for the term "Hispanic" versus "Latino" as a group descriptive. The term "Chicano" is used in selective areas of the Southwest. In Cuban American circles, the term Latino has not been generally accepted – they prefer either Cuban American or Hispanic.

Latinos began to find their political voice in the 1960s, in protests and campaigns against abuse and discrimination. In Crystal City, Texas, for example, a large agricultural Mexican American community boycotted a school that was supported primarily by Mexican parents but run by Anglos. The Mexicans' demands for educational reform proved powerful enough that Anglo officials ceded control to a new Hispanic superintendent. The incident drew national attention, and was a source of inspiration for the creation of the La Raza Unida Party in Texas, spearheaded by fiery Jose Angel Gutierrez. Before that incident, there had been scattered protests, but nothing so astonishing as this. It gave Latinos a glimpse into their untapped power, and provided a model for future activism.

One of the most powerful voices ever to emanate from the Latino community was that of Cesar Chavez, who managed to effect enormous

Science

Luis Walter Alvarez, 1911-1988

Luis Alvarez received the Nobel Prize in 1968 in physics for "the discovery of a large number of resonance states, made possible through his development of the technique of using hydrogen bubble chamber and data analysis." Specifically, his research made it possible to record and study the short-lived particles created in particle accelerators. Early in his career, Alvarez worked concurrently in the fields of optics and cosmic rays. He is the co-discoverer of the "East-West effect" in cosmic rays. During World War II, he was responsible for three important radar systems – the microwave warning system, the Eagle high altitude bombing system, and a blind landing system of civilian as well as military value. This noteworthy Latino scientist also held research positions at the Massachusetts Institute of Technology (MIT) and University of Chicago.

change through nonviolent protest and an unflagging dedication to Latino farm workers. "When people say nonviolence won't work, they are really saying that they cannot organize," Chavez once told an interviewer. "When we speak nonviolence, we must seek a way and a means of showing people how to become better and more effective organizers."

Chavez was relentless in his pursuit of fair wages and decent pay for migrant workers. He organized the United Farm Workers union, staged successful boycotts, and eventually won farm workers the guaranteed right to collective bargaining. "We do not hate you or rejoice to see your industry destroyed," Chavez wrote to E.L. Barr, Jr., then-president of the California grape and tree fruit league. "We hate the miserable system that seeks to keep us enslaved and we shall overcome and change it, not by retaliation or bloodshed, but by a determined nonviolent struggle carried on by those masses of farm workers who intend to be free and human."

Latinos had won. They finally staked out their own piece of ground. Trouble was, it was out in the fields. It was hot, dirty, back-breaking work. It was not glamorous. It was not sexy. And it certainly wasn't lucrative. But it was a beginning. It might even have felt a bit like retribution, that deliciousness of bringing the powerful California growers to their knees.

It was a success in marked contrast to the Zoot Suit Riots in the early 1940s, when sailors on shore leave in Southern California formed roving gangs to hunt down and beat Mexican American teens dressed in the fashionable zoot suit. Young Chicano boys were stripped of their suits while citizens and the local police stood by. After months of fighting and inaction on the part of city officials, military shore patrols quelled the riots and restricted sailors from Los Angeles city streets. City officials finally took action, ordering mass arrests and banning the wearing of zoot suits.

The military may have stopped the sailors from acting out their prejudice, but it didn't stop discrimination against the Hispanic community. It would take years before Latinos found their way into better paying jobs, until they moved from the fields to the city, had children who actually graduated from high school or college, until they started businesses, ran companies, or ran for office.

You will read in this book that Latinos' population growth rate is off the charts, that Hispanics already outnumber African Americans as the largest ethnic minority group in this country, and will surpass them in consumer spending in the next five years. Hispanics outpace all other groups in terms of growth, and comprise the most active work force among American workers. You will discover that the work force in the next 10 years and the taxpayer base in the next 20 years will be predominantly Hispanic. If you are like most people, you'll say, "So? What does that have to do with me?" In a word: everything.

If you're a business owner, you're wondering how you can get a piece of that $700 billion. If you're a presidential candidate, you're courting the Latino vote. If you're a banker, you're wondering how you can cash in on the $30 billion in remittance money, and wondering what is a *matricula consular?* If you're a real estate agent, you're translating brochures into Spanish so you can tap into Latinos' emerging middle class and its desire to own a home. If you're a business with a website, you're creating bilingual web pages because you know there are 14 million Latinos online, half of whom are actively seeking Spanish-language content. If you're a marketing firm, you're devising multicultural strategies to reach this attractive, multi-faceted market.

But if you're Hispanic, you're probably not thinking about these things at all. You're cleaning someone's house or mowing their grass. You're checking groceries or having lunch with your fellow office workers. You're studying for your college finals or grinding out that dissertation. You're in court, fighting for your client, or you're in your office at the clinic, hoping that baby's mother understood your directions and will give her the right dose of the medicine you just prescribed. Maybe you're teaching at an Ivy League university, presiding over criminal cases, or hoping that this election will be the one that sweeps you into office.

In short, you're living your life, paying bills, and putting food on the table. Saving for a house, or putting money away for a college education – either yours or your children's. What you're *not* doing is thinking about that $700 billion you and your neighbors will spend this year. You're also not thinking about being a member of the largest, youngest, and fastest-growing ethnic minority in the country. It's not that you're disinterested. You're just busy.

You're certainly proud of the strides Latinos have made, of their ability to transcend prejudice, racism, and discrimination to become labor leaders, politicians, artists, musicians, athletes, and business leaders. Sometimes you do wonder, though, why there aren't more than a handful of Latinos in positions of power. When you hear a business owner say his work force is 30 percent Hispanic, you wonder if that 30 percent is mopping the floors or signing the paychecks. You wonder if Hispanics comprise 30 percent of his customers, or if Hispanic vendors provide 30 percent of his supplies. Is there proportional Latino representation in today's businesses?

Yet the demands of life bring you back to your reality. Will you graduate from college? Will your children graduate from college? Will you ever be able to buy a home? Pay for health care? Get a better paying job with benefits and a retirement plan? It's hard to think about 40 million people spending $700 billion, much less figure out what it has to do with you, or how you can benefit, how you can contribute, or what part you'll play in the evolution of the Latino community.

Science
Ellen Ochoa

A renowned astrononaut with NASA since 1991, and the first Hispanic woman in space, Ellen Ochoa has completed three shuttle missions, logging more than 719 hours in space, and undertaken a leadership position as payload commander aboard the Atlantis for mission STS-66. Her passion for research, engineering, and space exploration has been evident throughout her professional career. Prior to joining NASA, Ochoa earned her doctorate in electrical engineering at Stanford University, and later at Sandia National Laboratories and NASA. Ochoa investigated optical systems for performing information processing, and is co-inventor for three patents for optical engineering systems.

RIGHT BEFORE OUR EYES is the story of the Hispanic people and their evolution into an economic and political powerhouse. It is an attempt to freeze, just for a moment, this fast-moving story long enough to ask: Who are these people? What are their values? What do they think? What do they buy? How do they vote? At nearly 40 million strong in 2004, are they a cohesive group?

RIGHT BEFORE OUR EYES is a compendium of the latest facts, figures, and analyses collected from Hispanic demographic experts, marketing professionals, academics, and media reports. It attempts to paint a picture of a community whose people come from many countries, each with their own culture and traditions. It details the contributions of Hispanics who helped make the U.S. a political, military, and economic leader. It examines the role Latinos had in building the American Dream, and asks why they have been systematically prevented from sharing it. It asks why Hispanics have no meaningful representation at the executive levels of business, education, law, politics, and policy.

For the first time in recollection, the Hispanic community finds itself positioned to wield a new kind of power. How will they use it? Will they put their money behind politicians who speak to issues important to them? Will they use their economic power to demand a retail market that serves their needs, in a language that is comfortable for them? Will they use their voting power to keep politicians who respond to their needs, and to get rid of those who don't? Will they use their sheer critical mass to demand educational reform, upgraded facilities, better teachers, and textbooks that present the Hispanic story with as much truth and vigor as other minorities? Will they demand affordable health care and medical insurance for their families? Will they push for the enforcement of laws that protect minorities from discrimination in the housing, banking, and labor markets?

RIGHT BEFORE OUR EYES paints a vivid picture of the changes and far-reaching impact this influential group will have during the first half of the 21st century. Ultimately, though, **RIGHT BEFORE OUR EYES** presents a call to action to Latinos and non-Latinos alike. This nation has changed and will continue to change, and this book identifies what must be done to ensure a future of shared destiny and proportional representation at all levels of society. We examine:

Leadership – Where is Latino representation at the highest levels of business, government (elected and appointed), medicine, research, in Ivy League schools, and in the courtroom? Given their advanced educational levels, why aren't today's Latinos sitting on the boards of Fortune 100 companies? Is there a way to create a kind of annual report that evaluates Hispanic representation on corporate boards and at the management level?

Politics – Can Hispanics unify on political issues in a way that will benefit their community? Can they wield their collective clout to put in place representatives who speak to their concerns? Policy can be shaped by the electorate, and the Latino community, armed with as many as 6 million registered voters in 2004, has the potential to wield its political power. Is this community willing to effect changes that will be crucial to the development and progress of Hispanics? Are politicians willing to listen?

Media – How does the media portray Latinos? Does the Latino child see on television or in print the faces of her kind? Do mainstream radio, television, and print media speak to issues important to Hispanics? Does it give them information in their own language? In America today there are more than 140 Spanish-language television stations, 600 Spanish-language radio stations, and about 550 Spanish-language magazines, newspapers, and websites. It is an industry all its own, and it exists within the largest English-speaking country in the world. What would happen if the majority of the 40 million Hispanics – those who are bilingual, plus another 6 to 8 million illegal residents – bypassed the mainstream media entirely, choosing instead to patronize outlets that actually served their needs?

Community Solidarity – Latino individuals and community organizations, from the local to national levels, must develop comprehensive reports on local- and corporate-America's Latino initiatives, including business and corporate sponsorships of community events, and developmental and educational initiatives.

Education – Parents and students, high schools and college associations must convince PTAs, textbook publishing companies, bookstores, and those responsible for curriculum development, that education must speak more loudly about the contributions of Latinos in matters of history, art, education, culture, politics, technology, and leadership. They must identify or create foundations and grant programs that support new Latino initiatives, and that provide funding for facilities and materials. A greater emphasis must be placed on the support of early education for all of America's children, with a focus on schools that have a high concentration of Latino children. This would include an increased number of better qualified teachers, improved school facilities, stronger ties with parents, and increased representation on school boards.

Economics – How do Latinos spend their money? Parents and their children alike must be more aware of how and where they spend their dollars. Do the stores and corporations they patronize hire local people, and funnel their profits back into the community? Should the Hispanic consumer press local businesses for improved hiring practices at all levels; for financial support of and partnerships with local school systems; for economic development of area businesses?

Healthcare – One out of every three U.S. Hispanics does not have medical or dental insurance. That rate is just as high, if not higher, for Latino youth under age 18. Mexican foreign-born workers accounted for almost 70 percent of all work-related accidental deaths from 1995 to 2000 – the third leading cause of death among Hispanics. It is a health care crisis that, left unaddressed, will only get worse, leaving the sick and injured untreated and costing taxpayers billions in health care costs.

RIGHT BEFORE OUR EYES is a work about one of America's oldest and yet newest national minorities. A proud, hardworking community that will continue to add to the richness and beauty of the American landscape.

RIGHT BEFORE OUR EYES points out the need to develop the potential that exists in this community.

We must foster a sense of shared destiny; cultivate the conviction that we each own a piece of the American Dream. It is not solely the province of white America. We do not deserve less because our parents or our grandparents may have been immigrants. Our claim to a life in the U.S. is as valid, and certainly older, than that of any other American.

CHAPTER TWO

A Proud History with Bittersweet Results

The history of Hispanic influence on the American culture dates back five centuries, before the Mayflower docked at Plymouth, before New York was a city, and before the founding fathers of our country had even inked the Declaration of Independence. Spanish explorers had traversed most of the Southern states from Florida to Texas, discovered Lake Michigan in the north, trekked down the Mississippi River, crossed New Mexico, Colorado, Nevada, and Arizona, and claimed the California coast extending as far north as Vancouver Island – all more than 60 years before Britain settled its first so-called "permanent colony" in Jamestown, Virginia, in 1607.

St. Augustine, Florida, founded in 1565 by the Spanish admiral Pedro Menéndez de Avilés, served as Spain's military headquarters in North America for the rest of the 16th century, and remains to this day the oldest city on the North American continent.

The Hispanic imprint is indelible in the Spanish-inspired architectural style of the South and Southwest – low-pitched roofs, rounded and red-tiled, stucco siding painted in pastel colors, spiral columns and pilasters, patterned tile floors and walls, arched doors and windows, open courtyards, decorative railings, carved stonework. It is a style that blends the architectural traits of the

Mediterranean with New World influence.

The Spanish influence also can be heard in the names of American cities and states, like Boca Raton, Cape Canaveral, El Paso, Las Vegas, Los Angeles, San Antonio, San Francisco, Santa Fe, California, Colorado, New Mexico, Montana, Nevada – all named by Spanish explorers.

More than merely naming cities, regions, and places, the early Spanish explorers introduced the Old World to a smorgasbord of foods discovered in the Americas, including corn, potatoes, tomatoes, bell peppers, chili peppers, vanilla, pumpkins, cacao (chocolate), squash, pineapples, and avocados. They discovered the drug quinine, which came from the bark of the cinchona tree, and was used by Indians in South America to treat malaria.

The Spanish Catholic clergy followed on the heels of the explorers, establishing scores of Catholic missions that became the foundation of legal and moral traditions in the New World. Among them was Father Junipero Serra, who would become a pioneer in the fight for the rights of Native Americans.

Despite these many contributions, the historical legacy of Hispanics in America has been marginalized, starting with a series of events during the 1800s.

After the province of Mexico gained its independence from Spain in 1821, this new nation, with its own northern provinces (California, Arizona, New Mexico, Colorado, Texas, Nevada, and Utah), began grudgingly conducting free trade with a United States government that was fixated on achieving Manifest Destiny. In 1836, Texas won its independence from Mexico and became a republic. Nine years later Texas was annexed into the U.S.

Following its victory in the Mexican War (1846-1848), the U.S., under the terms of the Treaty of Guadalupe Hidalgo, was awarded the territories that today make up California, Nevada, Utah, New Mexico, Arizona, and parts of Colorado and Wyoming. This vast area was home to approximately 80,000 Mexicans, most of whom were granted U.S. citizenship. Many of these Hispanic communities also held communal land grants that the Spanish crown had given them decades before in an attempt to encourage the settlement of New Spain's northern territories. Under the terms of the Hidalgo treaty, as well as those of the Gadsden Treaty (1853), the civil and constitutional rights of

Mexicans in these newly acquired lands were to be protected. Instead, the Treaty of Guadalupe Hidalgo proved to be a monumental turning point that would have adverse ramifications for Hispanics in the Southwest for decades to come.

Mexicans residing in these newly acquired territories suddenly discovered they had been rendered second-class citizens by their new American government. Historical records offer numerous accounts of how racism toward Mestizo- and Indian-origin Mexicans and Mexican Americans created a legacy of bitterness and conflict that lasted well into the 20th century and, some would say, still lingers in certain segments of U.S. society.

Historical records also show that U.S. officials at all levels of government often ignored the treaty agreements that ostensibly gave Mexican Americans the same rights as all U.S. citizens. Some historians say these political, legal, and banking rings conspired to deprive Mexican Americans of their lands.

In the years after the Mexican War, as more and more settlers came in search of land on which to grow crops and raise livestock, and the demand for land soared, Mexican American landowners repeatedly were forced to confirm their claims in U.S. courts. The process was time-consuming, relentless, and expensive, forcing many to either secure loans or sell large tracts of land to pay court costs. Many Mexican Americans were unable to communicate with the English-speaking judges, and did not understand the U.S. court system. As a result, they often were jilted out of their legitimate claims to the land.

By the late 1800s, most Mexican Americans had lost their land deeds and become tenants or workers on land that now belonged to Anglo Americans. The two groups lived in segregated neighborhoods in towns and cities, each with its own schools, stores, and places of entertainment. Mexican Americans called their sections *barrios*, the Spanish word for neighborhoods.

Until about the 1890s, the immigration of Mexicans to the United States was barely discernible. Jobs on large cattle, sheep, cotton, and vegetable farms attracted some Mexicans to Texas, but not in great numbers. Increased Mexican immigration began with the development of railroad systems in both Mexico and the U.S. The rail systems afforded a large number of Mexican workers— many of them from deep within Mexico—relatively inexpensive and readily accessible transportation to the border and to certain regions of the United States.

By 1900, it is estimated that about 127,000 Mexican-born people migrated to the U.S., pushing the overall Mexican American population in the Southwest to upward of 600,000. As would occur throughout much of the 20th century, Mexican immigrants or seasonal workers from Mexico, along with the native Mexican American population, became the primary source of labor for large commercial agricultural businesses, especially in Texas and in the fertile valleys of central and southern California. In addition, jobs in the mining industries of California, Arizona, Colorado, and New Mexico attracted thousands of skilled Mexican miners and unskilled laborers.

The early 1900s saw a sharp increase in the number of Mexican immigrants as economic conditions in Mexico worsened. In 1910, the Mexican Revolution broke out, pushing Mexico into years of political and economic chaos. The revolution sparked a wave of immigration that continued until the 1930s; between 1910 and 1930 almost 700,000 Mexicans fled Mexico for a life in the United States.

During the 1920s, Mexicans accounted for more than 10 percent of all U.S. immigration. Most settled in the Southwest, where they took jobs in factories and mines, or on railroads, farms, and ranches. In 1917, when the U.S. entered World War I (1914-1918), as many as 200,000 Latinos – the majority of them Mexican Americans – volunteered for service.

The wartime economy provided new opportunities for those Mexican Americans left behind, as key manufacturing industries replaced the hundreds of thousands of able-bodied American citizens who had joined the war effort. Until World War I, Latinos were employed primarily in agriculture, mining, and the railroads. Now many moved to construction jobs, and settled in Midwestern industrial cities, such as Chicago and Detroit, to work in skilled positions in the rapidly growing automobile and meat-packing industries.

Despite these gains, Mexican Americans suffered discrimination in jobs, wages, and housing. They organized labor unions and took part in strikes to obtain higher wages and better working conditions. Mexican Americans also formed civic groups to deal with these problems. In 1929, a number of groups merged to form what today is the oldest Hispanic civil rights organization in the U.S., the League of United Latin American Citizens (LULAC).

Business
Prudencio Unanue, 1886-1976
Born in 1886, Prudencio Unanue immigrated to New York in 1916, where he studied business, and worked for a customs agency. Recognizing there was a deficiency in suppliers of authentic Spanish food ingredients, he opened Unanue, Inc. in 1936, which later became Goya Foods. The Goya Foods business continues to flourish to this day, noted for its production of quality Spanish foods, innovative advertising and marketing, and active community involvement. Headquartered in New Jersey, Goya Foods, Inc. has factories throughout the U.S., Puerto Rico, the Dominican Republic and Spain.

Despite the economic opportunities afforded by World War I, historians note that both Mexican nationals and Mexican Americans suffered significantly at the hands of the predominantly white society even in the best of times.

During economic downturns after World War I, the U.S. government, which had been eager to attract workers from Mexico during boom times, began as a matter of policy to make the task of crossing the border – let alone becoming a naturalized U.S. citizen – much more difficult.

There are numerous accounts during the post-World War I years of vigilante groups targeting Mexican nationals and Mexican Americans alike with vicious and often fatal attacks, blaming them for depriving Anglo Americans of jobs.

The height of this anti-Mexican sentiment came during the Great Depression, when President Herbert Hoover blamed economic conditions on the presence of Mexicans. As a result, the U.S. Immigration and Naturalization Service (INS) rounded up an estimated 600,000 Mexicans, including U.S.-born Mexican Americans and their American-born children, and repatriated them to

Mexico. The deportations represented about a third of the total Mexican population living in the United States during the early 1930s.

It was the largest mass deportation of any ethnic group in U.S. history. There are those who believe this sordid period in American history had much to do with Mexican Americans being further marginalized and kept at low educational levels, allowing for little economic mobility.

In addition to the humiliation of repatriation, restaurants began refusing to serve Mexican Americans. Public swimming pools, restrooms, drinking fountains, and theaters were often segregated. Mexican American schoolchildren were often forbidden to speak Spanish in schools, and were sometimes punished severely for doing so.

Despite these abuses, when World War II erupted in 1941, an estimated 500,000 Hispanics – again, the vast majority of Mexican descent – either enlisted or were drafted into the military. Their courage and valor on the battlefields of World War II led Latinos to earn proportionately more service awards than any other ethnic group, including 13 Medals of Honor, the highest decoration an American combat soldier can receive.

By war's end, as Latino veterans returned to America, there began to develop a different set of expectations than those that prevailed before the war. Emboldened by their military service, these veterans and thousands of their fellow Latinos who had contributed to the war effort on the home front demanded their full due as citizens who fought shoulder-to-shoulder with Anglos throughout the war. The struggle against rampant discrimination in employment, housing, and education became a major rallying cry for Latino organizations, associations, and legal defense committees. LULAC, the American GI Forum (formed after World War II), and other organizations were advocates for Latinos. These organizations began to systematically challenge racist practices. LULAC sponsored initiatives that succeeded in desegregating schools in southern California in 1946. It also played a key role in desegregating public schools in Texas, where the organization had already established a solid record of success prior to World War II. Under pressure from Mexican American groups, some Arizona schools ended segregationist practices in the 1950s.

The outbreak of WWII also saw the creation of the *bracero* program, which was designed to supplement the labor shortages in the U.S. with temporary Mexican workers. The program extended far beyond World War II, though. Established in 1942, it ran for 22 years. At its peak in the mid-1950s, it granted as many as 450,000 temporary working visas to Mexican agricultural and railroad workers in a single year.

Although the program was a steady source of cheap labor, it cemented the practice of recruitment and deportation, with one major exception: Even after the U.S. Congress refused to expand the program in 1964, Mexican participants opted to stay with their families in the U.S., many of them illegally.

Over the course of the *bracero* program, an estimated 4.5 million Mexican citizens were legally hired for work in the United States, primarily in Texas and California. The program also helped to establish what became a common migration pattern – Mexican citizens entering the U.S. for work, returning to Mexico for a brief time, and returning to the U.S. during the next seasonal period, creating the so-called "circular migration pattern."

The harsh treatment of Mexicans under the *bracero* program – poor wages, squalid living conditions, exposure to pesticides – led the late farm labor activist Cesar Chavez to create the United Farm Workers of America in 1966, a union that today represents thousands of fruit and vegetable workers throughout the Southwest. Over the years, the union has forced numerous growers to sign contracts that improved worker's wages, health care, working, and living conditions.

The mid-1900s also brought the first major waves of Puerto Ricans to the U.S. Puerto Rico had been a U.S. possession since 1898. Its people had been U.S. citizens since 1917, which allowed them unrestricted access to the U.S.

Between 1940 and 1960, more than 545,000 Puerto Ricans migrated to the U.S., primarily to New York City, to look for jobs. By 1960, almost 70 percent of Puerto Ricans living in the U.S. were living in New York's East Harlem, which still has the largest Puerto Rican population of any U.S. city (about 40 percent of all Puerto Ricans live in the New York metropolitan area).

Cuban immigration picked up sharply during the late 1950s after Fidel

Castro came to power. Before the mid-1950s, only a few thousand Cubans immigrated to the U.S. each year. After Castro took over in 1959 and announced the restructuring of Cuban society, the number of Cuban immigrants increased dramatically – mainly middle- and upper- class Cubans who found Castro's plans threatening to their way of life. Between 1959 and late 1962, about 200,000 anti-Castro Cubans immigrated to America, most of them settling in South Florida around Miami.

In October 1962, commercial air flights between Cuba and the U.S. were suspended. Nonetheless, about 50,000 Cubans entered the United States in the next three years, thousands of them secretly sailing away from Cuba in small boats. In 1965, the U.S. and Cuban governments agreed to set up an airlift between Cuba and Miami. The airlift, which operated until 1973, brought about 250,000 Cubans to Florida.

Until 1994, the U.S. welcomed Cuban immigrants, believing they were victims of Castro's oppressive regime. Many of the first Cubans to flee Castro's dictatorship in the early 1960s were well-educated and from well-to-do families. The government granted political asylum to these immigrant Cubans, and offered federal help to qualified applicants in finding homes and jobs.

Another major influx of Cuban immigrants came in 1980 with the *Marielitos*. In the spring of 1980, Castro opened the Cuban port of Mariel to thousands of refugees, who were intent on braving "wind and tide" to cross to Key West, Florida, there to find the promise of a new life in the U.S. Numbering about 125,000, the *Marielitos* were a group the Cuban government wanted out of the country – political dissidents, unskilled workers, criminals, and the mentally ill. The government allowed the *Marielitos* into the U.S., even though officials had not expected such large numbers of people, and were at first unaware that criminals were among them. Some of the criminals subsequently were placed in prisons, many were rehabilitated and released; a few were returned to Cuba.

In 1994, thousands of Cubans, intent on escaping the poverty of their homeland, set out for southern Florida on small boats and rafts. But soon after this influx began, President Bill Clinton announced the U.S. would not accept any more of the refugees. This policy was designed to avoid the cost of settling large numbers of refugees in Florida. Many of the Cubans were stopped at sea by U.S. ships, and taken to a U.S. naval base at Guantanamo Bay on Cuba's coast.

Nearly two-thirds of all Cuban Americans live in Florida today, with more living in Miami than any other U.S. city. Large numbers of Cubans also live in suburban towns outside Miami and in Tampa, on Florida's west coast. Although the Little Havana section of Miami remains the center of the Cuban American population, many have moved into the city's more affluent neighborhoods. Some of Miami's most successful businesses are owned and operated by Cuban Americans. New York City, Los Angeles, and Chicago also have significant Cuban populations.

Community Advocacy
Tomás Rivera, 1935-1984
A noted champion of the Latino/Hispanic community, Tomás Rivera received international acclaim as an educator, author, and scholar. Rivera held a firm belief that Latinos would play an integral role in establishing a better life for their community through involvement in government, business, and education. In 1979, Rivera was named chancellor of the University of California, Riverside campus, becoming the first Mexican American chancellor in the U.S. In commemoration of Tomás Rivera's life work, The Tomás Rivera Policy Institute was established in 1985 at the Claremont Colleges in Claremont, California. This nationally recognized nonprofit organization remains steadfastly devoted to nonpartisan policy analysis of issues affecting the Latino/Hispanic communities. It is regarded as the premier policy think-tank for Latino issues in the United States.

People from Latin America continued to immigrate in large numbers to the United States between 1970 and the late 1990s. It is important to note that

Hispanics accounted for more than one-third of all *legal* immigration during that period. Still, illegal immigration inflows have been high. It is estimated that there are 6 to 8 million undocumented workers (most from Mexico) working and living in the United States.

In the 1980s and 90s, large numbers of Hispanic immigrants have come from war-torn countries in Central America, including El Salvador and Nicaragua. Many are children and teenagers whose parents were killed or have disappeared. One opinion is that these Central Americans should be granted political asylum in the United States. But U.S. officials maintain that many of them are motivated more by economic than political concerns.

As Hispanics move into the 21st century and look back on more than 500 years of Latin American history in the U.S., some might argue that much of it has been bittersweet and at times even unsavory – lost Spanish land deeds, vigilantism, discrimination, farm labor abuse, indiscriminate mass deportations, housing prejudice, and political exclusion. Despite these barriers, Hispanics are a proud people who remain resolutely optimistic about their future. They have seen what can be achieved, even without the benefit of a level playing field:

Science: Luis Alvarez in 1968 won the Nobel Prize in physics for his work with subatomic particles. He also helped develop microwave beacons to help aircraft with ground-controlled landings.

Aerospace: In 1986, Costa Rican-born Franklin Chang-Díaz, the first Hispanic astronaut, roared into space. He was followed by astronaut Sydney Gutiérrez. In 1993, Ellen Ochoa became the first Latina in space.

Art: Luis Jimenez is a Texas-born artist who creates monumental sculptures that celebrate his Mexican heritage. Using "low-brow" materials, including fiberglass and plastic, he creates satirical comments about American life. He also works in bronze. His images depict modern pop culture, including the stereotypical American West.

Architecture: Andres Duany is an architect and town planner whose work focuses on the creation of New Urbanism, which seeks alternatives to suburban sprawl and urban disinvestment. A Cuban American, Duany is internationally recognized for the design of Seaside, Florida, and has completed designs for more than 200 town, downtown, and regional areas.

Medicine: Puerto Rican-born Dr. Antonia Novello was the first Hispanic and first woman to become Surgeon General of the U.S. in 1990. Prior to becoming Surgeon General, she was deputy director of the National Institute of Child Health and Human Development, where she took a special interest in pediatric AIDS. Since leaving office in 1993, Novello has served UNICEF, the United Nations' children's health organization, as special representative for Health and Nutrition.

U.S. Military: Admiral David G. Farragut, the first full admiral in the U.S. Navy and a hero during the Civil War. He is remembered for his famous battle cry, "Damn the torpedoes! Full speed ahead!" In 1964, Admiral Horace Rivera, a Puerto Rican, became the Navy's first Hispanic four-star admiral. In 1982, General Richard E. Cavazos, a Mexican American from Texas, became the Army's first Hispanic four-star general. Cavazos served with the 65th Infantry Regiment during the Korean War, earning a Distinguished Service Star in June 1953 as a lieutenant during frontline battle action. In July 1998, Louis Caldera, a Mexican American and West Point graduate, became the highest-ranking Hispanic to hold office in America when he became secretary of the Army, serving until January 2001.

Politics: In 1928, Octavian A. Parasol was the first Latino to serve in the United States Senate, representing New Mexico. The second Hispanic to be elected to the U.S. Senate was Dennis Chavez, also from New Mexico, who served from 1935 until his death in 1962. The first Latino to serve in the U.S. Congress was Joseph M. Hernandez, elected in 1822 in what was then known as the Florida territory. U.S. Senator Joseph M. Montoya won the 1964 Senate election to complete the term of Senator Chavez. During his 11-year career in the Senate, Montoya served on the Appropriations Committee, the Public Works Committee, the Joint Committee on Atomic Energy, and most memorably, the Senate Select Committee on Presidential Campaign Activities, popularly known as the Watergate Committee. He served until 1977. There have been 25 Latinos, including eight women, elected to the U.S. Congress. Bill Richardson was elected governor of New Mexico in 2002 by the largest margin of any candidate since 1964; in 1997 he served as the U.S. Ambassador to the United Nations and in 1998 was appointed as secretary of the U.S. Department of Energy. In 1989, Ileana Ros-Lehtinen, a Cuban American from Florida, became the first Hispanic woman elected to the U.S. Congress; she is serving her eighth term. In 2002, Loretta and Linda Sanchez became the first sisters to be elected to Congress at the same time. Loretta was elected in 1996; Linda was elected in 2002.

Education: Jaime Escalante may be the nation's most famous teacher. Virtually single-handedly, he turned Garfield High School in East Los Angeles into a symbol of academic achievement in mathematics. Escalante was the subject of the 1988 movie *Stand and Deliver,* which dramatized his efforts to help underachieving Latino students beat the odds and pass an advanced placement calculus test for entry into college. Lauro Cavazos was the first Hispanic to serve as U.S. Secretary of Education from 1988 to 1990. He was also the first Hispanic to hold a U.S. cabinet post, and served as president of Texas Tech University. Tomás Rivera was the first Latino to serve as a president of a university. He was chancellor at the University of California, Riverside. Rivera also wrote *"y no se lo tragó la tierra"* (And the Earth Did Not Devour Him), which is considered a milestone in Mexican American literature. Eduardo Padron is president of Miami Dade Community College, nationally recognized as the largest and one of the best community colleges in the country. It is the nation's top producer of associate of arts degrees.

Union Organizing: In 1966, Cesar Chavez formally organized thousands of Mexican farm workers into the United Farm Workers union, the first farm labor organization formulated in the U.S. to improve wages, work and living conditions, and other employee benefits. He and Dolores Huerta, another UFW leader, helped organize national boycotts in the 1960s and 1970s that drew support from as many as 17 million American citizens. Huerta remains active in the UFW today.

Pulitzer Prizes: In 1984, the *Los Angeles Times* won the Pulitzer Prize Gold Medal for Meritorious Public Service, the most prestigious of all the Pulitzers, with an all-Latino team of 13 editors and staff writers and two staff photographers; the project involved an in-depth examination of Southern California's growing Latino community. In 1987, Andres Oppenheimer, a staff writer for the Miami Herald, won a Pulitzer for national reporting on the U.S.-Iran-Contra connection. In 1993, Liz Balmaseda, of the Miami Herald won a Pulitzer in the category of commentary for her columns. And in 2004, Cheryl Diaz Meyer of the Dallas Morning News won in the category of breaking news photography for work depicting the violence and poignancy of the war in Iraq.

Music: The flamboyant Tito Puente was probably the most beloved symbol of Latin salsa jazz. A trained musician, Puente kept his music remarkably fresh over more than five decades, combining mastery of rhythmic nuance with old-fashioned showmanship. The Cuban-born songstress Celia Cruz, the "Queen of Salsa," was one of Latin music's most respected vocalists. A 10-time Grammy nominee who sang only in her native Spanish, Cruz received a Smithsonian Lifetime Achievement award, a National Medal of the Arts, and honorary doctorates from Yale University and the University of Miami. The musical team of Emilio and Gloria Estefan formed the Miami Sound Machine, one of the most successful Latin crossover acts of the 1980s that became popular worldwide. Tejano music artist Selena became a vocal sensation in the 1980s and 90s. Hailed as the Latina Madonna, the flamboyant, sexy stage performer's musical style crossed cultural boundaries, making her enormously popular in Latino communities across North America. Carlos Santana is one of rock music's greatest guitarists. In 1999, Santana's album "Supernatural" won eight Grammys, tying him with Michael Jackson for the most Grammys ever won in a single year. Altogether, Santana has won 10 Grammys in a career spanning almost 40 years.

Sports: Lee Trevino (golf), Chi Chi Rodriguez (golf), Joe Kapp (football), Jim Plunkett (football), Tom Flores (football), Nancy Lopez (golf), countless boxers (including Oscar de la Hoya), and baseball stars (Alex Rodriguez, Manny Ramirez, Sammy Sosa, Miguel Tejada, Rafael Palmiero, among others) have reached superstar status as a result of their athletic prowess.

Movies: At the birth of the movie industry, Hispanic actresses like Myrtle González and Beatriz Michelena were some of the most popular draws in silent films. Hispanic stars in the 1920s and 30s included Dolores del Río, Lupe Vélez, and Ramón Novarro. The decades of the 1940s, 50s, and 60s headlined stars like Rita Hayworth, Fernando Lamas, Anthony Quinn, and Rita Moreno (the only artist to win an Oscar, Emmy, Tony, and Grammy).

Television: In the 1950s, Desi Arnaz, the famed Cuban bandleader, created his own television production studio. He introduced the "three camera" technique (now a staple of the industry), and was the first to use film to preserve TV shows for reruns. The *I Love Lucy* series he produced remains one of the most-watched series of all time.

It is clear that Hispanics are not without role models. The people named here, along with a host of others, have made significant contributions to the American landscape. Their achievements lend hope and promise that more will be achieved in the future. To be sure, there is quality in this list. But it also lacks the depth of talent and numerical strength that should be representative of a people who have been here for more than five centuries. And while it heralds the capabilities and contributions of the Hispanic culture, it does not speak well of the limited level of inclusion America has afforded Latinos. If it did, we would not be speaking about the "first Latino…" or the "first Latina…" to attain a level of success or achievement that Anglos reached decades ago.

It is a good list, a proud list. But in many respects, it represents the exception rather than the norm. Will the same be true in 20, 30, or 40 years? There are scores of talented, educated Latinos today who are betting it won't – Latinos who are banking on the promise that they will be regarded as exceptional rather than the exception.

CHAPTER THREE

An Untold Story of Duty and Honor:
Latinos in the United States Military

There is one stellar fact that is irrefutable and truly underscores the depth of Hispanic commitment and patriotism, and that is the military record of the Hispanic soldier. It is as old as the United States, dating back to the American Revolution. Since that time, Hispanics have participated in virtually every U.S. military conflict with honor and valor.

In the eyes of many Americans, there is perhaps no other act of U.S. citizenship that exemplifies patriotism, honor, and duty more than donning a military uniform in the service of this country. The image of the indomitable American soldier standing resolute with weapon in hand, ready to defend this country, has long characterized what it often takes to live as a free American.

This has not been lost on Hispanics. In fact, arguably the most notable contributions Latinos have made to America have been in the military service. Sadly, that story has been largely untold or relegated to footnote status. Yet it is a rich, colorful account of Latino participation that most historians have failed to explore or chronicle.

For many Hispanic veterans, their story has been as overlooked as that of the Latino workers who harvest our fruits and vegetables, landscape our rose gardens and lawns, take our dinner orders, serve our food, and clear away the dishes at thousands of restaurants; Latinos who mop, dust, and vacuum millions of offices; Latinas who tend and cook in homes and help raise other people's children in countless upscale neighborhoods. These Hispanics are transparent; American society tends to look through them, not at them. They know someone does the work. They just don't know or care who it is.

The chronicles of Latinos in the military have been similarly treated. The eyes of an American nation have never seen this group's profound commitment to the ideals of duty, honor, and valor. Their military track record should speak for itself, but many Latinos, including Hispanic military veterans, believe their story has either been ignored or given short shrift.

"For 228 years of American history, the Hispanic has always been there. We have fought in wars and served during peacetime. We have died for this great nation. We have suffered tremendous losses and countless wounded. We have won the highest honors that Congress can bestow on heroes. And yet our place in history will never go down as that of other groups," said retired Major General Alfred A. Valenzuela, who left the U.S. Army this summer after almost 34 years of service.

"It could be because we are so patriotic – if there is such a thing. It could be because our work ethic and our values teach us to go from being an individual to working within a collective sphere of teamwork that we don't concern ourselves with the record of what happened. We just do it the old-fashioned way. We perform when it's important and deliver at every turn. We don't brag about our ventures or our successes. We just slug away thinking that that is what's expected of us, and we never think much about the glory that success brings for us in the military ranks. But that's not what we're about, that's not who we are. We are quiet warriors, quiet heroes. We are brought up to do our mission and move on."

Today's U.S. military is one of the nation's largest employers of Hispanics, with about 110,000 service personnel, representing 8 percent of the country's total military forces. In many respects, it has been America's ultimate common denominator, the equalizer that puts all men and women, regardless of their walk of life or social or economic circumstances, on equal footing. Or as one newspaper account altruistically put it, "…a more egalitarian and racially harmonious society, one in which prejudice is trumped by meritocracy, discipline, and the need to get along to survive."

Valenzuela agreed, but only to a point. "I would say that if we hadn't been so quiet we'd have three times as many Medal of Honor recipients (there are 42), we'd have three times as many generals. We would have what the blacks have because they raised hell at one point, and they are now a force to be reckoned with (within the military)."

The same has been true in the documentation of Hispanic military history, said Valenzuela. "We have been our own worst enemies. We in essence do it to ourselves. We didn't document and capture the history of who we are. We just can't seem to find the audacity of words to say, hey, wait a minute, I can stand up and be counted."

It is this kind of modesty, which is characteristic of Hispanics, that explains, at least partially, why the story of one million Latino veterans who are living testaments of duty and country has gone untold. "...Latino veterans don't tend to be chest-thumping braggarts about their war experiences or tours of duty," said Valenzuela.

Hispanics celebrate Veterans Day, Memorial Day, and the Fourth of July much like any other veteran's group, but find it difficult to relate their wartime

---

Community Advocacy
Cesar Chavez, 1927-1993
Cesar Chavez founded the United Farm Workers (UFW) in 1962, formalizing his commitment to the improvement of living and working conditions for farm laborers. His non-violent advocacy included the five-year Delano Grape Strike, frequent fasts, and, in 1966, a 340-mile march from Delano to Sacramento. Chavez's efforts significantly reformed American agriculture. He was also a U.S. Navy veteran of WWII, and was awarded an honorary doctorate from Arizona State University, the only school to award him such distinction. In 1994, one year after his death, Chavez was awarded the Presidential Medal of Freedom.

exploits, or to recount the images and faces of close friends lost in battle. For many of today's Latino veterans, there is a quiet solitude and an unwavering private pride in having answered the call.

And, yet, there are critics who belch on with inane fears about the so-called "browning of America," about how "the persistent inflow of Hispanic immigrants threatens to divide the United States into two peoples, two cultures, and two languages." It is these critics who do not understand that while Latinos may be bicultural and bilingual, their military record shows they have always been single-minded in their loyalty to the American flag.

Has there ever been an Anglo soldier who cared that his flank was protected by a tan-skinned sharpshooter, or that the man who fell mortally wounded beside him spoke his dying words in Spanish?

But there are always, of course, those who do care, like Samuel P. Huntington, chairman of the Harvard Academy for International and Area Studies, and co-founder of *Foreign Policy* magazine. In his book, *Who We Are*, Huntington wrote, "Unlike past immigrant groups, Mexicans and other Latinos have not assimilated into mainstream U.S. culture, forming instead their own political and linguistic enclaves—from Los Angeles to Miami—and rejecting the Anglo-Protestant values that built the American dream. The United States ignores this challenge at its peril."

He added: "The single most immediate and most serious challenge to America's traditional identity comes from the immense and continuing immigration from Latin America, especially from Mexico, and the fertility rates of these immigrants."

Huntington claimed Latinos were not assimilating into American culture, and actually argued that Mexico – presumably including Mexican Americans – could one day attempt to reclaim territories it lost to the United States during the 19th century, including Texas and most of the Southwest.

The peril of Huntington's raving lies not in a presumed lack of Hispanic assimilation, but in his narrow, condescending viewpoint – however scholarly – and the daft notion that Anglo-Protestant values alone imbue one with the exclusive right to the American dream.

Try telling the descendants of the 200,000 Latinos who served in World I, or the 500,000 who served in World War II, the almost 150,000 who fought in the Korean War, the 100,000 who engaged in the Vietnam War, or the 110,000 Latino men and women who, as of March 2004, were in the U.S. Armed Forces, that they haven't served, fought, or died for some piece of that American dream.

How much more assimilated does a community have to be before they are accorded legitimacy in American culture? What is the litmus test for such acceptance? It certainly has not been in the U.S. military, where recruiters, eager to put these "warriors" in uniform, tout the benefits of education, job opportunity, overseas travel, adventure, and a heightened sense of personal pride.

Try telling the Latino families, descendants, and recipients of 42 Medals of Honor dating back to the Civil War – 21 of which were bestowed posthumously – that their ancestors' heroics didn't earn them a smidge of the American dream. Try telling the families of the fallen Latino soldiers, whose names are etched on the Vietnam War Memorial in Washington D.C., that their loved ones represent any less dedication to America than any other ethnic group. Try telling the thousands of Latino soldiers who served in the Gulf War that their non-Anglo-Protestant backgrounds are a peril to the country. Tell this to the Latino soldiers in Iraq and Afghanistan as they patrol the frontlines in towns whose names their mothers and fathers can't even pronounce.

Does it matter to Iraqi and Al-Qaida forces, as they squeeze off rounds from a semi-automatic weapon or build a bomb in the trunk of a car, that Latino soldiers represent America's second culture or speak its second language? What matters is that they are killing soldiers who represent the United States of America. How fast does one have to assimilate into American mainstream culture before becoming eligible for enemy gunfire?

Valenzuela attended the funerals of 22 Hispanic soldiers who were felled in the Iraq War, four of which were non-U.S. citizens – the four were awarded their American citizenship posthumously. Valenzuela said the reaction from the soldiers' parents was nothing short of incredible.

"When you help bury them, the parents will come up to you and tell you, *"murio por su patria adoptada"* ("He died for his adopted country"). One mother came to me and said, 'Look general, if we could give you another child, we would give him to you because our son died a hero. He died protecting this country and kids of the future. And he didn't die in a drug deal or a car accident.' Man, what a powerful statement," Valenzuela said.

Riding the wave of patriotism that swelled after the September 11, 2001 terrorist attacks on the World Trade Center and the Pentagon, President Bush in the summer of 2002 issued an executive order that decreed non-citizens with permanent resident status could join the armed forces and earn their American citizenship after honorably completing three years of service. A subsequent law passed in November 2003 reduced the length of service to one year before applying for U.S. citizenship.

As a result, an estimated 40,000 non-citizens joined the U.S. Armed Forces, about a third from Mexico and other Spanish-speaking countries. The rest came from China, Vietnam, Canada, Korea, India, and other countries. Non-citizen soldiers represented about 2.5 percent of the 1.4 million men and women on active duty in the summer of 2003. Another 20,000 non-citizen permanent residents serve in the Reserves and the National Guard.

Aside from earning their American citizenship, many of these non-citizens were motivated by the prospect of post-service financial aid for education and improved job opportunities. Some were even lured by the idea of traveling to faraway lands.

As of June 2004, Latinos represented one out of every eight American soldiers killed in Iraq. About 690 had been wounded there. Among the first to be killed in the Iraq War was U.S. Marine Lance Cpl. Jose Gutierrez of Guatemala City, Guatemala, in Central America. According to published reports, Gutierrez was killed by "friendly fire" when his fellow soldiers saw him running out of a building they had already secured, and mistook him for an enemy soldier. Other non-citizen Latinos who lost their lives in the Iraqi War came from Mexico, Cuba, Colombia, the Dominican Republic, Bolivia, and Argentina.

Valenzuela, who since his retirement has launched a foundation to help at-risk Latino youths in San Antonio, gives high praise to non-citizen soldiers. "You take an immigrant who just crossed the damn border, and if I go in the army and he goes in the army at the same time, well, that soldier is going to work twice as hard as those who are second, third, and fourth generation because they want it worse than we do," Valenzuela said. "That kid cares about the country. He's got a green card. He knows he's got a vote. He knows that he's got to get his kids educated. And he knows that he's got to participate to make it."

While the social scientists may argue the merits of assimilation, acculturation, and linguistic crossover, and the speed at which these transformations are progressing, there is one indisputable fact that cuts across all of those debates. If one accepts the argument that enlistment in any branch of the U.S. Armed Forces represents the ultimate act of pledging allegiance to the United States of America, no group has stepped up to "walk the walk" more than Latinos.

From 1992 to 2001, while the overall strength of the U.S. military dropped by 23 percent, from 1,775,000 to 1,369,000, the number of Hispanics in uniform grew by 30 percent, from 90,600 to 118,000, according to a report by the Pew Hispanic Center in March 2003. During that period the total number of successful enlistments fell by 11 percent while successful Hispanic enlistments increased by 31 percent. (Successful enlistments represent the net number of people who make it from recruitment to actual service; for example: 100 enlisted, 80 qualified.)

Hispanics represented only 7.6 percent of enlistments in 1992, but jumped to 11.3 percent in 2001. At the same time, Latino accessions to the ranks of commissioned and warrant officers increased from 2.8 percent of the total to 4.7 percent. This included a significant increase in the number of Hispanic officers earning commissions at the nation's military academies, from 1.7 percent to 4.1 percent of the overall total, according to the Pew study.

A substantial portion of increased enlistments happened during the watch of former Secretary of the Army Louis Caldera, a West Point graduate, who in

July 1998 became the highest-ranking Hispanic to hold office in the U.S. government.

Faced with recruitment challenges when he took the post, Caldera, together with the Army's Chief of Staff, General Eric K. Shinseki, set into motion their vision of a more versatile and deployable force. Caldera made expanding high school outreach programs and improving educational opportunities for soldiers a cornerstone of the Army's efforts to reverse recruiting and retention shortfalls, while increasing soldiers' skills and technical competencies.

He is credited with, among other things, spearheading the Army of One recruitment campaign, and launching a number of initiatives that became widely popular among both recruits and soldiers. In 2000, he launched two initiatives, the College First Enlistment Program and GED Plus, the Army's high school completion program.

The College First program allowed college students to enlist in the Delayed Enlistment Program, and continue their college education while receiving a monthly stipend. The recruit then entered the Army at an advanced rank, provided the recruit had earned at least 30 college credits. Recruits also were eligible for a $3,000 College First enlistment bonus.

Because all branches of the armed services require a high school diploma or a GED (General Educational Development), Caldera created the GED Plus Program, which provided Army sponsorship to applicants seeking a high school diploma or an equivalency certificate in order to enlist.

Caldera also created the Army University Access Online, an education program that enabled soldiers to earn college and graduate degrees while serving. He promoted the expansion of the Junior ROTC program to hundreds of high school campuses nationwide, and spearheaded Army sponsorship of Operation Graduation, a three-year public service advertising campaign designed to increase high school graduation rates among at-risk youth.

"I knew I had big recruitment problems that I had to deal with on my watch," said Caldera, who served as secretary from 1998 to 2001, and today is president of the University of New Mexico. "The Army was viewed as being mired in its Cold War past and needed to have a different rationale. (It) needed to change, literally to be transformed. It had to evolve a different set of capabilities, a different sense of purpose if it was going to be relevant in the war and in the fight for resources."

The eldest son of Mexican immigrants, Caldera was born in El Paso and raised in Whittier, California. He graduated from West Point in 1978, and served as a commissioned officer in the Army from 1978 to 1983, rising to the rank of captain. He earned a law degree and an M.B.A. from Harvard University in 1987.

When he took over as secretary in 1998, he was confronted by Army recruiters who maintained that their recruiting efforts of Latinos – particularly among Latino college students – were on par with, if not slightly higher than, the average college graduation rate among Hispanics. Their explanation, Caldera said, was "utter nonsense. I said that's not what we are going to be. We are going to double our goal for recruiting Hispanics because it should not be based on what the Hispanic college-going rate is today. It should be based on what the Army is going to look like 20 years from now."

About 38 percent of the country's total armed forces are made up of ethnic minorities, with blacks (22.5 percent) and Hispanics (9.5 percent) accounting for the vast majority. But among the nation's officer corps, ethnic minority officers account for only 16.7 percent of all officers (blacks 8.3 percent and Hispanics 3.8 percent). The percentages shrink – and are increasingly worse for Hispanics – when one tallies the number of generals and admirals.

A report from the Pew Hispanic Center showed that in 2001 blacks represented 5.1 percent of all generals and admirals; Hispanics accounted for a mere 1.5 percent, more than three times lower than their fellow black officers. In 2003, Hispanics represented just under 5 percent (4.8 percent, or 3,262 officers) of the Army's entire officer corps. According to the U.S. Army, there were only seven Hispanic generals out of a total of 307 in 2004.

Caldera said the lack of Hispanic representation in the military is a situation that merits attention and action, particularly since ethnic minority groups will represent half of the nation's population within the next 30 to 40 years, and presumably make up a substantial portion of military personnel. Can the U.S. armed forces be optimally effective when the highest-ranking commanding officers are predominantly white, and 50 to 60 percent of the rank and file is minority personnel?

"It is in the Army's and the military's best interest to maintain their political support," Caldera said. "It's very important that they pay attention to diversity (or) it will be a recipe for tension. There will be this perception that a non-Hispanic officer corps controls the lives of a Hispanic force who they don't relate to. And when you're sitting there saying, 'I am taking these troops to Iraq and a bunch are going to get their butts whacked,' well, it is a huge disconnect."

Caldera believes the Army must take a different approach as it recruits Latinos. "One, we are using the wrong metric. We are thinking about it in terms of the college-going rate, and we need to do better than that. Two, we are at the wrong schools. We need to open our ROTC programs in schools that have high minority enrollment. Three, in the enlisted ranks, why aren't we recruiting enough Hispanics? Because Hispanics don't have high school degrees, so we need to work on that."

But is a high school diploma an appropriate guideline to determine who makes the best soldier? Caldera and Valenzuela both believe that such a requirement shuts out a great number of Hispanic candidates who want to be soldiers.

"We have to educate the powers that be – is it that only high school graduates make the best soldiers?" Caldera said. "Hispanics have the highest interest in military service. You poll all the youth groups. 'Would you be interested in joining the Army?' 'Are you thinking about joining the Army?' Hispanics have the highest interest in military service, the highest enlistment rates, the highest re-enlistment rates, and the lowest attrition rates. So they make great soldiers."

The U.S. Army only allows about 15 percent of its total enlistments each year to have a GED. Valenzuela believes the Army should expand the scope of its GED program to recruit more Hispanics into the military. Army reports of GED enlistments in 2003 showed that only 491 Latinos enlisted via the GED requirement, representing 6.7 percent of the total GEDs.

"Why can't we accept more GEDs? The National Guard has a challenge program for kids who are at risk, who get thrown out of high school and then they volunteer to go to that boot camp, and they come out with a GED," he said. "The kid who comes out of that boot camp ought to have every damn right that a high school kid does, particularly a high school kid who can't read or write either. We just have to change with the flow. I think because we are at war, we should make outright changes because war dictates when we need more good men and women."

The military began requiring a high school diploma after the Vietnam War, when a number of soldiers with substandard educational backgrounds were killed in action. "The military began to use high school diplomas as a proxy for quality," Caldera said. "They said 'Who are the drug users? Who are the discipline problems? Who are the ones who fail and leave the Army? We have to get them out of here.' They sold the country and sold the Congress on it, saying a high school diploma equals quality."

Caldera's and Valenzuela's argument to loosen recruitment requirements comes at a time when the military is facing increasing pressure to step up recruitment efforts in an attempt to shore up manpower demands for missions in Iraq and Afghanistan. The Pew report showed Hispanic soldiers were a good investment. The report showed that "survival rates" for Latinos – the percentage of personnel who remain in the service after their initial four-year enlistment – were highly prized by the military's high-ranking brass. It was a clear indicator that the branches of the military are reaping the benefit of the training and specialization of its Latino soldiers.

The Pew Hispanic Center study also showed retention rates among Hispanic troops were higher than average in 1992, and increased during the subsequent 10-year period when the nation's military numerical strength dropped significantly. For example, enlisted personnel who joined the service in 1992 had an overall survival retention rate of 36.9 percent. Among enlisted

---

Politics
Henry G. Cisneros
In 1992, Henry Cisneros was nominated by former President Bill Clinton and confirmed unanimously by the U.S. Senate to serve as the Housing and Urban Development (HUD) secretary. As HUD secretary, Cisneros was responsible for administering fair housing and economic development activities and programs. He began his career as an administrative assistant in the San Antonio, Texas, office of the city manager, and later went on to become a White House Fellow, assistant to the Secretary of Health Education and Welfare Elliot Richardson, and a member of the San Antonio city council. In 1981 he became the first Hispanic mayor of a major American city (San Antonio). Cisneros earned his graduate degree in public administration at Harvard, and his doctorate in public administration from George Washington University.

---

personnel who joined in 1996, the rate was 40.4 percent for Latinos compared to 37.3 percent for the military overall, three points higher than it was only four years earlier.

A similar trend was true for the Latino officer corps. Among officers commissioned in 1992, 82.1 percent of Latinos were still on active duty four years later, compared to 83.9 percent overall. When the rates were compared again four years later, the data showed 86.8 percent of commissioned Latino officers were still on active duty, while the overall percentage of the officer corps dropped almost four points, to 82.9 percent.

But while the retention trend among the Latino officer corps is a strong positive trend, the path to the ranks of general and admiral remains tightly bottlenecked. Valenzuela takes a more pessimistic view than Caldera.

"We will never have more than (a handful of) Hispanic generals at the same time, never. You want to mirror the demographics and the population in the United States – that's what you want to do. But I don't think we will ever be there at the percentages that will make it equitable," Valenzuela said.

"Look, it takes thirty years to grow a general," Caldera said. "We need them coming out of ROTC today for the coming demographic shift of tomorrow so that when the officer corps becomes thirty percent Hispanic, we have a prayer of fielding five percent, seven percent, eight percent, ten percent Hispanic officers. So we have to do it now based on the future force, not based on the current force."

In the last 40 years, only two Hispanics have risen to the top ranks of the U.S. military profession. In 1964, Admiral Horacio Rivero, a Puerto Rican, became the Navy's first Hispanic four-star admiral. In 1982, General Richard E. Cavazos, a Mexican American from Texas, became the Army's first Hispanic four-star general.

This was not lost on either Caldera or Valenzuela. It is a picture that is not made any prettier now that Caldera and Valenzuela are on the outside looking in. And there are more challenges on the horizon. At the time of this printing, America's military commander in Iraq, Lt. Gen. Ricardo Sanchez, a Mexican American from South Texas, relinquished his command over a 160,000 military force after the debacle at Abu Ghraib, the Iraqi prison where American soldiers were accused of abusing Iraqi detainees.

It provoked a worldwide outcry, and very likely ended Sanchez's chance at a fourth star. According to press reports, many believe Sanchez was a scapegoat for the mess at Abu Ghraib. The 31-year veteran, who grew up in poverty in Rio Grande City, Texas, indicated publicly that he probably would continue serving for a couple of years before resigning.

As secretary of the Army, Caldera was responsible for the department's annual budget of nearly $70 billion. He led a workforce of more than a million on active duty, plus the National Guard, Army Reserve soldiers, and 270,000 civilian employees, and had stewardship over 25 million acres of land. Valenzuela, who grew up on the streets of San Antonio, was in charge of the Army's U.S. Army South, which included responsibility over all regions south of the United States to the tip of South America. He was popular among his junior charges, and was particularly noted for his mentorship of Latino officers.

Two of the three highest-ranking Latino officials are gone – Sanchez presumably will leave in two years. At a time when the recruitment numbers among Hispanics are on the rise, the absence of three key Latino leaders who had a far-reaching impact up and down the ranks is likely to be felt for years. It begs the questions: Where will the leadership come from? And what, if anything, will the military do to fill the void?

A One-Man Army

Goodbye, my dear parents, he told us, just as he left,
He said don't remain sad for I will be back real soon.
I am a real Mexican and I am not afraid to die.

He said goodbye to his fiancée, and to his brothers, too,
He gave a hug to his mother and he also gave one to me.
He asked for our blessing and of that of the Lord.

Dear Lord, you know what a mother has suffered
To give her son his life, she even risked her own life,
In exchange for that of my son, I offer you my very own.

From "Ballad of a Soldier's Father"
Translated from Spanish lyrics;
Author Unknown; Vietnam War

Battlefield heroes don't wake up one morning and suddenly announce to the world that they're going to do something heroic that day. There often is no rhyme or reason as to the circumstances. Yet, in a split second of time – between life and death – heroes summon up something that separates them from fellow soldiers, that extra bit of adrenaline, that extra bit of intestinal fortitude, daring, if you will, that changes them for the rest of their lives.

The battlefield exploits of Ret. Col. Joseph Rodriguez fall into all of those categories. It has been more than 53 years since that day in May 1951 when Rodriguez's life did indeed change. He has never discussed the details of the battle that earned him the Medal of Honor. But there were witnesses, and the Army has citations recording the events of that day.

The withering barrage of enemy gunfire from the five fortified emplacements situated up on the high, rugged terrain was raining down on Company F, Part of the American 7th Infantry Division. The initial assault on the North Korean stronghold by the 3rd Platoon had stalled only 60 yards from where the Communist hostile force was commanding the crest of the hill just north of the village of Munye-ri. The 3rd Platoon had attempted to scale the hill but had been repulsed by the same five enemy gun placements three different times, suffering heavy casualties each time. It was now 2nd Platoon's turn.

The 2nd soon ran into the same hail of gunfire that had ripped up the 3rd Platoon. Fanned across the crest of the hill, the five emplacements continued to command the high ground as they raked the American troops with unrelenting fire from automatic weapons and small arms. Worse yet, the enemy had begun to roll grenades down the hill at the American soldiers hunkering down behind whatever cover they could find. They couldn't retreat. They couldn't advance. Twenty-two-year-old Pfc. Joseph Rodriguez was fully aware of the odds against the 2nd Platoon, but as the assistant squad leader, he figured something had to be done soon. Otherwise his men would be shot to pieces. Leaping to his feet, Rodriguez dashed the 60 yards up the fire-swept slope, and in the next few harrowing moments transformed himself into a one-man army.

After lobbing grenades into the first enemy emplacement with deadly accuracy, Rodriguez raced around the left flank. He silenced a second automatic weapon with two grenades, and continued his assault to the top of the peak, where Rodriguez wiped out two more foxholes. After reaching the right flank, he tossed grenades into the remaining emplacement, destroying the gun and annihilating its enemy crew.

As the smoke cleared from Rodriguez's assault, the American troops below began to cautiously make their way up the slope. When they reached the top, they found the bodies of 15 enemy dead. Miraculously, Rodriguez did not have a scratch on him.

It was an incredible display of valor for this skinny American-born boy, whose Mexican parents had immigrated to America to scratch out a living in the citrus fields around San Bernardino, California. The sixth oldest of 18 children, Joseph Rodriguez's deeds became legendary.

As a result of Rodriguez's "intrepid actions" that day on May 21, 1951, military reports stated that "the defense of the opposition was broken, the enemy routed and the strategic strongpoint secured."

Rodriguez's "unflinching courage under fire" earned him the Medal of Honor, the highest military decoration an American soldier can earn on a battlefield. Rodriguez's heroic actions would affect him the rest of his life. And it had all taken place less than eight months after he was drafted into the U.S. Army in October 1950.

His Medal of Honor citation stated that "Rodriguez distinguished himself by conspicuous gallantry and intrepidity at the risk of his life above and beyond the call of duty in action against an armed enemy," and that his courage and devotion to duty "reflect the highest credit on himself and uphold the honored traditions of the military service."

But the quiet, unassuming Rodriguez didn't figure he'd done anything special. He didn't even think himself a hero, even as fellow soldiers shook their heads in amazement at what he had done in those few deadly minutes. Rodriguez was impervious to the attention and the "scuttlebutt" that was being spread around – there was talk about important medals and decorations and the like. "It didn't matter to me," he said.

To Rodriguez, his actions that day were no different than those of any good soldier under the same circumstances. He bought none of the heady talk, preferring to keep his feet firmly planted on the ground. He had done his job, which was all that truly mattered.

He remembers his father, Jose, taking him aside just before reporting for duty to the U.S. Army. "Joe, don't be afraid," his father said. "You're a man."

"You know it was that machismo (thing). But it stuck with me," Rodriguez said recently. "Dad didn't pamper us. So he gave me his blessing before I left and those were his parting words. It worked."

Several months after Rodriguez's assault on the enemy hill, he realized there must be a kernel of truth to the rumors of medals and citations, when his superiors ordered him to pack up his personal belongings – he was heading back to the United States. The only thing that mattered to him was the large bundle of love letters he received almost daily from his girlfriend, Rose Aranda. Those letters kept his spirits up while in combat. There was little else to pack.

He was put on a small plane and flown to Tokyo, Japan, where the military checked the impressionable Rodriguez into the elegant, four-star Imperial Hotel. "Boy was it fancy," he recalled. "I mean I'd never been in one like that before. I mean top of the line. I thought, I can take this. One day I'm on the battlefield and the next I'm in one of the richest hotels in the world. It was quite a dream."

After cleaning up, getting a haircut and new clothes for his trip home, Rodriguez was taken to meet General Matthew B. Ridgeway, who in 1951 succeeded General Douglas MacArthur as commander of United Nations forces in Korea and of the allied occupying forces in Japan. "I paid a call to the top dog of the area," he said proudly.

Rodriguez did not recall Ridgeway saying anything about the Medal of Honor. "To me, it didn't mean anything at the time," he said. His mind was on other things. There was one last thing to do before heading home. He went to the local PX in Tokyo where he did some shopping. "I picked up a couple of rings, an engagement and a marriage ring with intentions of proposing to Rose, which I did shortly after I arrived (home) at Thanksgiving."

Back in San Bernardino, Rodriguez got a hero's welcome as local newspapers ran banner headlines and stories of his heroics. "I went along and went wherever they wanted me to go," he recalled. "I did a lot of interviews. By that time everybody seemed to know what had happened … I was going to Washington to meet the President. They played it up real good. I was grateful."

He remembered his father "was popping his buttons with pride. He was proud. He didn't say much, but I could tell. It made me feel good. It made me feel good that I made him feel good."

Before heading back to Washington to receive the Medal of Honor, Rodriguez proposed marriage to Rose, who accepted but insisted that he also ask for her father's permission and blessing, which he did.

There was yet more good news. "I was promoted to Sergeant First Class," he said.

On January 29, 1952, in Washington, President Harry S. Truman presented Sergeant First Class Joseph Rodriguez with the Medal of Honor, making him one of 42 Latinos awarded the nation's highest military citation. In a sense, Rodriguez was one of the lucky ones, as half of the 42 were presented their medal posthumously. Further, U.S. military records show that of the 131 who received the Medal of Honor during the Korean War, 94 (about 72 percent) received their citation posthumously.

Rodriguez said his wife, Rose, was "flabbergasted because of all the publicity. She was included in everything. She was in a daze. We just tried to keep our cool."

Following the medal ceremonies, Rodriguez was assigned to an army reservist base in San Bernardino, where he figured he'd complete his military service, return to school, and build on the two years of college work he'd already completed toward an architect's degree. But seeing that jobs were tight in the San Bernardino area, Rodriguez mulled his choices in the Army.

In mid-1952, Rodriguez was convinced by a senior officer to pursue a career as an officer. After passing a physical, taking an aptitude test, and going before a review board, Rodriguez was promoted to second lieutenant, and was sent to Fort Belvoir, Virginia, to an Engineer Officer Basic Course.

The career move paid off. Eventually he ascended to the rank of colonel in what became a 30-year military career that included assignments in Panama, Bolivia, Puerto Rico, Vietnam, Korea a second time, and Argentina. "My wife moved 22 times in that time we spent together in the military," said Rodriguez, who constantly used the word "we" when talking about his career. "I always talked with Rose about things. She was involved in every decision."

Rodriguez's career influenced both his sons, Charles and Lawrence. Charles Rodriguez graduated from the U.S. Military Academy at West Point in 1975, and today is a brigadier general in the Texas Army National Guard. He works as assistant vice president at the University of Texas Health Sciences Center in San Antonio. Lawrence Rodriguez attended the U.S. Air Force Academy in Colorado Springs, but eventually decided to pursue other interests. Today, he is a vice president with Wells Fargo Bank in Carson City, Nevada. Joe and Rose Rodriguez also have a daughter, Karen, who is married to a retired Army nurse.

After retiring from the Army in 1980, the elder Rodriguez worked 10 more years at the University of Texas at El Paso as director of facilities. He retired in 1990. Today, he spends a good part of his week answering letters from school children from all over the country, as well as adults who request his photograph and autograph. "I guess it's like a fan club," he said.

Looking back on his three decades of service, Rodriguez is blunt about the military life. "Rose was very patient," he said. "But it's like I told one of the youngsters in one of the letters, the military is not for everyone. Some children and wives cannot adjust. They cannot adapt. They cannot accept the rigors of military life. But we were very fortunate that our family did."

Although he talked about his military career, Rodriguez refused to discuss the events that earned him the Medal of Honor. The details of that day are personal, he said. "I haven't talked about it since then. I'm not about to start now."

His son Charles remembered that as a youth he was curious when family or friends asked, "Do you know what your Daddy did? You know that we think highly of him?" Charles's memories were more vivid of the times his father would "point things out, the small but important things about leadership." He never directly asked his father about his war experiences until recently, when "I started to capture some of these things with audio tape interviews. But I didn't drill into the events of that day."

"It wasn't verboten. I suppose if I had asked him point blank he probably would tell me," he said. "It's just one of those things. He's been very open about lots of things he thinks and lots of things that have happened. But he's never volunteered anything in detail about that day. If it's something he doesn't want to tell me about, that's fine. There's so many other things that he can tell me about. We just leave it alone and let the citation speak for itself."

Charles was in junior high school before he even read his father's Medal of Honor citation. "And then it was just in passing because I really didn't get the meaning of words like valor and courage. It read like an action comic book. I couldn't figure out how that could be Dad. To me, he was just Dad."

Despite his decorated military career, Rodriguez never pressured his sons to follow in his footsteps. "I think he's always been clear from the very beginning that everyone has to pick his own direction in life. And if it's the military, great, and if it means being a business person, then that's great too," Charles said. "Just make sure that it's honest, hard work. And do your best at it. He would always say, at the end of the day, the Army has been good. And if you don't know what else you want to do, the Army is an honorable profession to select."

A Proven Historical Record

The story of the Hispanic soldier in the U.S. military has been shunted aside by historians for more than 230 years. Of the thousands of books written about the exploits of American military forces, there is not a single title in any library that fully captures the historical breadth and role of the Latino soldier. A smattering of books have touched on specific events or individuals from one military conflict or another, but no author has yet to capture the story in its full historical context, with all its glory and in full military dress. This chapter offers a glimpse – albeit abbreviated – into a historical saga of involvement dating back to the birth of America. Why this rendering here? Because it is time, simply put, that Latinos and Latinas receive their due in this most quintessential of American experiences.

The American Revolution

Prior to the outbreak of the American Revolution in 1775, most of what is the United States today west of the Mississippi was part of Spain, including Mexico. In 1777, Bernardo de Gálvez was the Spanish governor of the Louisiana Territory. Although Spain did not enter the war as an ally to the 13 colonies until 1779, Governor Gálvez had been secretly providing aid to General George Washington's army by allowing tons of goods, including money, medicine, cloth, guns, gunpowder, and other military supplies, to be moved up the Mississippi River to the American patriot forces in the north.

According to historical accounts, Gálvez corresponded directly with Patrick Henry, Thomas Jefferson, and Charles Henry Lee. He responded to their pleas by securing the port of New Orleans so only American, Spanish, and French ships could move up and down the Mississippi River.

Once Spain did enter the American Revolution, Gálvez put together a patchwork army of Creoles, Choctaw Indians, free African Americans, and his own Spanish regulars totaling about 1,400 men. He was ordered by Spanish King Carlos III to conduct an aggressive campaign against the British along the Gulf Coast. He focused primarily on the Mississippi waterway, the most critical thoroughfare to northern points. In the fall of 1779, Governor Gálvez's army took to the field, and marched on British-held forts at Baton Rouge, Manchac, and Natchez, essentially severing Britain's access up the Mississippi for the remainder of the war.

In March 1780, following a month-long siege with land and sea forces totaling more than 2,000, Gálvez, captured the British stronghold of Fort Charlotte at Mobile. The climax of his Gulf Coast exploits came in 1781, when he successfully directed a multinational force of more than 7,000 during a two-month-long joint land and sea attack on Pensacola, Florida, at that time the British capital of West Florida. One historian called the battle "a decisive factor in the outcome of the Revolution, and one of the most brilliantly executed battles of the war."

After capturing Pensacola, Gálvez in 1781 captured the British naval base at New Providence in the Bahamas. He was making preparations to invade Jamaica when General Washington's forces captured Yorktown, bringing an end to the Revolutionary War. After the war ended, Gálvez was among those who helped draft the terms of the treaty with Britain. He was later cited by the American Congress for his critical role during the struggle for America's independence. For his role in the war, Gálvez was memorialized in Texas, when the city of Galveston was named in his honor.

The Battle of the Alamo

Considered one of the most dramatic events in Texas history, the battle of the Alamo gave birth to one of the most famous rallying cries for Texas independence. The notorious defeat at the hands of Mexican General Antonio Lopez de Santa Anna has been glorified and depicted in numerous films and books as that of a small courageous band of 180 Texans braced against incredible odds as they attempted to fight off a Mexican army of about 2,000 on March 6, 1836 at a San Antonio mission. Santa Anna was intent on crushing the Texas revolt. He ordered the Texans at the Alamo to surrender. They would be given no quarter if they refused. The defenders of the mission, including William B. Travis, David Crockett, and James Bowie, decided to fight.

The Texans held the mission for 12 days, taking positions behind inadequate defenses while waiting for reinforcements that never came. At the end of the 13th day, all 180 were killed. Their bodies were piled into a human pyre and burned. According to historical accounts, about 30 non-combatants, including women, children, and a few blacks, were allowed to leave the mission. Santa Anna reportedly lost about 600 men during the battle.

The battle at the Alamo marked a turning point in Texas' fight for independence as vengeful cries of "Remember the Alamo!" were shouted by *Texians* in every subsequent battle until Santa Anna and his army were finally defeated at the Battle of San Jacinto in April 1836. The Republic of Texas was born.

For decades to come, historians buried the fact that there were *Tejanos*

(Mexicans) who fought alongside their Texas brethren, including eight who were killed at the Alamo: Juan Abanillo, Juan A. Badillo, Gregorio Esparza, Jose Maria Guerrero, Damacio Jimenes, Jose Toribe Losoya, and Andres Nava, all residents of Texas.

What's more, it is a little-known fact that during the Battle of San Jacinto, there was a cavalry regiment of Mexican Texans commanded by Colonel Juan N. Seguin. It was Seguin who later re-entered San Antonio, and accepted the surrender of the Mexican forces there. After the war with Mexico, Seguin served in the Texas Senate, and was also elected mayor of San Antonio.

Three other Latinos merit a place in the annals of the Texas Revolution – Lorenzo de Zavala, Jose Antonio Navarro, and Jose Francisco Ruiz. Of the 59 men who signed the Texas Declaration of Independence in March 1836, these three *Tejano* freedom fighters were the only ones of Mexican ancestry who signed the document. Lorenzo de Zavala later became the first vice president of the Republic of Texas.

The Civil War

When war broke out between the states in 1861, loyalties among Latinos living in the United States were split between the two factions. Historians have found soldiers with such names as Gonzales, Garcia, Perez, and Sanchez who fought on both sides. About 2,550 Hispanics joined the Confederate military, while another 1,000 enlisted in the U.S. Army at the outset of the war. Altogether, about 10,000 Hispanics fought in the Civil War on both sides of the conflict.

During its early colonization of the New World in the 16th century, Spanish explorers established settlements throughout the South, stretching from present-day South Carolina on the Atlantic seaboard westward through Texas, the Southwest, and all the way to the Pacific coast. By the mid-19th century, with the Civil War on the horizon, Spanish influence was most prevalent in the Gulf states and the Southwest.

In Louisiana, local Hispanic soldiers supported that state's war efforts both at home and in the field. Nearly 800 Spanish soldiers in New Orleans were mustered into the "European Brigade," a home guard of 4,500 that kept order and defended the city, according to U.S. Department of the Interior's historical accounts. Other Louisiana regiments also recruited a number of Hispanics from the state. The brigades of Harry T. Hays (his brigade was popularly known as the "Louisiana Tigers,") and William E. Starke included native Louisianans of Anglo and Creole descent, plus men from Spain, Cuba, Mexico, and other Latin American countries, according to the Interior's records. Both brigades campaigned with General Robert E. Lee's Army of Northern Virginia in the battles of Antietam and Gettysburg.

Other Gulf Coast states also mustered Hispanics into the military. Interior records report that one Alabama company, the Spanish Guards, was made up exclusively of men with Spanish surnames, and served as a home guard for Mobile. Two other regiments, Alabama's 55th Infantry, which served in campaigns at Vicksburg, Atlanta, and Nashville, and Florida's 2nd Infantry, which fought at Antietam and Gettysburg, included a number of Hispanic soldiers, records show.

But Hispanic participation was most intense in Texas and the Southwest, including Arizona, California, and New Mexico. Probably more than anywhere else, loyalties among Latinos in the Southwest were bitterly split between the North and South. In Texas and New Mexico, there were resentful feelings that lingered from the Mexican War only 15 years before, when large Mexican territories like New Mexico, Arizona, Colorado, and California were ceded to the United States. Consequently, a number of Hispanics sided with the Union in defense of their newly adopted America, while other Latinos, who were tied politically and economically to the fortunes of Texas and the South, sided with the Confederacy.

Historical accounts note that many of these Latino volunteers served in integrated regular army or volunteer units. But there were also a number of all-Mexican American units with their own officers, particularly in the Southwest. In 1863, the U.S. military in California was given orders to raise four companies of native Mexican Americans from California. Renowned for their "extraordinary horsemanship," there were about 470 soldiers who served in the

First Battalion of Native Cavalry under the command of Major Salvador Vallejo. The First Battalion was stationed at locations throughout California and Arizona, guarding supply trains, chasing bandits, fighting off Confederate raiders and, in one instance, fending off a Confederate invasion of New Mexico.

In New Mexico, which was not yet a state, the Second Regiment of New Mexico volunteers was commanded by Colonel Miguel E. Pino. Six other independent militia companies were also formed. As in California, most of these units' members were Mexican Americans, as were their commanders. An estimated 4,000 served in New Mexico's volunteer army, including Hispanics like Lt. Colonel Manuel Chavez, who commanded a militia unit, and General Stanilus Montoya, who commanded a militia unit in Socorro County in the southern region of New Mexico, where the most intense conflicts with Confederate forces attacking from Texas took place.

In all of the bloody battles during the Civil War, the Confederate invasion of the New Mexico territory may appear as a minor drama. But the Confederate leadership harbored grandiose designs, including gaining control of the Santa Fe Trail and the gold mines of Colorado and California. These western-most campaigns represented a potential change in the course of the war. Instead, the Union factions, braced by the support of Hispanic Union patriots, were able to blunt the South's encroachment and drive them back to Texas.

In Texas, the Union raised 12 companies of Mexican American cavalry, consolidated into the First Regiment of Texas Cavalry. Most of the officers were non-Hispanic, although several *Tejanos* served as captains, such as George Trevino, Clemente Zapata, Cesario Falcon, and Jose Maria Martines, and as lieutenants, including Ramon Garcia Falcon, Antonio Abad Dias, Santos Cadena, and Cecilio Vela. Among the most prominent Latinos in Texas during the Civil War, however, was Colonel Santos Benavides, a former Texas Ranger who commanded the Confederacy's 33rd Texas Cavalry, and was the highest-ranking *Tejano* officer to serve in the Confederacy.

According to the Puerto Rican Hispanic Genealogical Society, Luis

Fenellosa Emilio, who was born in Salem, Massachusetts, of Spanish immigrant parents, was a company commander in the famous 54th Massachusetts ("Colored") Regiment. Fenellosa Emilio was one of the few officers who survived the charge on Fort Wagner, South Carolina, in July 1863. He later became the regiment's commander. His memoirs, entitled "A Brave Black Regiment," were the basis for the Academy Award-winning film, "Glory."

Admiral David G. Farragut

Probably no Hispanic figure stands out more as a hero of the Civil War than Admiral David. G. Farragut, who became the first officer in the U.S. Navy to be named an admiral, and who, by the end of the war, was in command of the entire federal fleet. Farragut goes down in Naval history as the officer who issued the famous order at the battle of Mobile Bay in 1864: "Damn the torpedoes! Full speed ahead!"

For his service and valor, Farragut was promoted to the rank of vice admiral, and is heralded as the most outstanding naval commander of the Civil War. In 1866, as thanks for more than 50 years of service, the U.S. Navy promoted Farragut to the rank of full admiral.

Civil War Medal of Honor Heroes

The first three Hispanics to ever receive the U.S. Medal of Honor for heroism earned their commendations during the Civil War – one was in the Army, the other two in the Navy.

Joseph H. de Castro

The 18-year-old Corporal Joseph H. de Castro of Company I, 19th Massachusetts Infantry was dug in with fellow soldiers, taking cover behind a low stone fence located directly in the center of the Union line at the battlefield on the southern outskirts of Gettysburg. At a few minutes after 1 p.m. on July 3, the third and last day of the bloodiest conflict of the Civil War, Confederate General Robert E. Lee unleashed an artillery bombardment unlike anything either seen or heard during the war. One witness reported that the massive cannonades produced "such a continuous succession of crashing sounds as to make us feel as if the very heavens had been rent asunder…"

Castro and six fellow soldiers from the 19th Massachusetts (Edmund Rice, John G.B. Adams, Daniel J. Murphy, Benjamin F. Falls, Benjamin H. Jellison, and John H. Robinson), who helped repulse portions of Pickett's Charge and captured the flag of 19th Virginia regiment, each were awarded the Medal of Honor for their bravery during the attack. On December 1, 1864, Castro officially received his Medal of Honor, making him the first Hispanic recipient of the nation's highest battle medal.

Two other Hispanic Union sailors earned Medals of Honor for their actions in battle during the Civil War. Ordinary Seaman Philip Bazaar was on board the U.S.S. *Santiago de Cuba* in January 1865 during the assault and capture of Fort Fisher, one of the last strongholds of the Confederacy. A native of Chile, Bazaar was one of six men from the fleet to enter the enemy works during the assault on Fort Fisher, carrying dispatches during the battle while under heavy fire from the Confederates. For these actions, Seaman Bazaar was awarded the Medal of Honor in June 1865.

A native of Spain, Seaman John Ortega enlisted in Pennsylvania and served as a seaman on U.S.S. *Saratoga*. Ortega was cited for his conspicuous gallantry during the action of the *Saratoga* on two occasions. His citation reads, "Carrying out his duties courageously during these actions, Ortega conducted himself gallantly through both periods. Promoted to acting master's mate." Ortega received his Medal of Honor in December 1864.

World War I

More than 200,000 Latinos fought in WW I, the majority of them Mexican American. At the time, immigration into the United States was significant. Of the almost 95 million in the U.S. population, about a third were recent immigrants, mostly from Europe. But there were also Latino immigrants coming in from Mexico and Latin America.

While Hispanics were eager to serve in the war, their entry into the military ranks was especially difficult due to their inadequate English, and because many also were subjected to racial discrimination. Latino recruits were often assigned by levels of language proficiency, and often were assigned bilingual officers who could communicate with them in Spanish.

One Latino who received the Medal of Honor posthumously during WWI was U.S. Army First Lieutenant David Barkley Cantu of Laredo, Texas, for his actions near Pouilly, France on November 9, 1918. During a battle along the Meuse River near Pouilly, Barkley and another soldier, both of Company A, 356th Infantry, 89th Division, volunteered to swim across the river to determine the enemy's exact position. Barkley succeeded in reaching the opposite bank despite enemy gunfire. Obtaining the necessary information, Barkley re-entered the river for his return. But before he could get across the river, he suffered paralyzing cramps and drowned in the chilly water.

In 1917, just before America entered the war, Puerto Ricans were granted their U.S. citizenship, and became eligible for military service. The majority of the 18,000 Puerto Ricans who were inducted into the island's six segregated infantry regiments were stationed in non-combat zones. Many of them were sent to guard the Panama Canal Zone while others were sent to Europe.

World War II

Historians have estimated that about 500,000 Latinos fought in World War II again, most of them Mexican Americans. About 53,000 were Puerto Ricans. There were 13 Latinos awarded the U.S. Medal of Honor during World War II. Four were awarded their medal posthumously.

Hispanics in the 11th Airborne Division's 511th Parachute Infantry Regiment, the 32nd Infantry Division's 127th Infantry and 165th Infantry regiments, and the 37th Infantry Division's 148th Infantry Regiment garnered at least one Medal of Honor in each regiment.

The 141st Infantry Regiment, part of the Texas National Guard's 36th Infantry Division, was a unit with a relatively large Hispanic contingent. The 141st was descended from the original 2nd Texas Volunteers, who fought during the Texas Revolution against Mexico in 1836. The regiment fought in Italy, France, Austria, and Germany, and in 361 days of combat suffered more than 1,100 deaths, about 5,000 wounded, and more than 500 missing in action. Three Latinos received Medals of Honor, while a host of others earned 31 Distinguished Service Crosses, 12 Legions of Merit, almost 500 Silver Stars, 11 Soldier's Medals, almost 1,700 Bronze Stars, and more than 5,000 Purple Hearts.

Another unit that fought with distinction during the war was the Arizona National Guard's 158th Infantry Regiment (Bushmasters). General Douglas MacArthur called the 158th Infantry, which consisted of large numbers of Mexican and Native Americans, "one of the greatest fighting combat teams ever deployed for battle." A part of the 45th Infantry Division, the 158th served with distinction in the southwestern Pacific Theater, fighting for 312 days and inflicting 3,000 casualties on the Japanese, while suffering about 500 casualties of its own.

Even though 350,000 Puerto Ricans registered for military service in World War II, only about 65,000 saw any battlefield action. Serving in mostly segregated units, including the Regular Army's 65th Infantry Regiment or the Puerto Rican National Guard's 295th and 296th Infantry regiments, large numbers were represented in support units, like the 245th Quartermaster Battalion, providing life-saving services and supplies. Additionally, about 200 Puerto Rican women served in the Women's Army Corps.

The Aztec Eagles

A seldom-recognized contribution to the war in the Pacific was made by the 201st Fighter Squadron from Mexico, known as the Aztec Eagles. This fighter unit was sent by Mexico after the U.S. declared war against the Axis Powers in June 1942.

The Aztec Eagles were a select group of 35 pilots and 300 enlisted men from all walks of life. They were sent to Pocatello Army Air Base in Idaho to train as a P-47 fighter squadron. They finished their training by early March 1945 with a superior record, and were then attached to the 58th Fighter

Group in the Philippines, where they began combat operations in June 1945.

Although the 201st was new to combat, its flight record compared favorably with that of veteran pilots of the 58th Fighter Group. They participated in bombing missions in Formosa, and supported troops from the 25th Division with bombing and strafing missions. During a 40-day period during the summer of 1945, the 201st flew 50 missions and 293 sorties. It dropped 181 tons of bombs and fired 104,000 rounds of ammunition. Seven of its pilots were killed in action.

On (U.S.) Veteran's Day, Carlos Foustinos, a former fighter pilot of the 201st, flies both a Mexican and American flag in commemoration of the men of the Mexican Fighter Squadron who fought and died in aerial combat along with Americans in the South Pacific. Faustinos flew approximately 25 missions, and recorded six Japanese Zero kills. His actions earned him the distinction of a flying ace. The Mexican government awarded him "La Cruz de Honor" (The Cross of Honor), the equivalent to the U.S. Medal of Honor.

Hero Street

In Silvis, Illinois, just west of Chicago, is a street about a block and half long with about 25 homes. It is called Hero Street. Formerly known as Second Street, the predominantly Hispanic neighborhood holds the distinction of sending more individuals to the armed forces than any other neighborhood of comparable size in the United States. According to the U.S. Department of Defense, Hero Street has sent more than 110 men and women into the military since World War II.

In May 1989, the city of Silvis and the Illinois State Historical Society erected a monument at one end of the street commemorating eight of the neighborhood's sons who lost their lives in World War II and the Korean War, as well as other veterans from the area. The eight men, Joseph Gomez, Peter Macias, Johnny Muñoz, Tony Pompa, Frank Sandoval, Joe Sandoval, William Sandoval, and Claro Soliz, grew up together in this close-knit community. Like their fathers before them, they worked for the local railroad. Six fought in World War II, and two fought in both WWII and the Korean War. All eight never came back.

The Korean War

At the outbreak of the Korean War, there were about 20,000 Latino soldiers serving in the armed forces. Over the next three years, about 148,000 served during the conflict. Of this total, approximately 60,000 were Puerto Ricans. During the Korean War, nine Latinos received the U.S. Medal of Honor for their heroism; two survived the war and seven received the Medal of Honor posthumously.

The Puerto Rican 65th Infantry Regiment

More than 4,000 men were in an all-Latino combat unit that served with distinction during the war, the Puerto Rican 65th Infantry Regiment, whose motto was Honor et Fidelitas, or "Honor and Loyalty." During the Korean War, this unit, nicknamed "The Borinqueneers" after one of the original Indian tribes of Puerto Rico, quickly won respect on the battlefield.

After arriving at Pusan, Korea, on September 20, 1950, the 65th saw heavy combat over the next three years, participating in nine major campaigns, including some of the fiercest fighting of the war. The 65th endured heavy ground fighting in Korea in some of the most mountainous terrain in the world, some during the harsh winter months when it was bitterly cold. The regiment is credited with killing 5,905, and capturing another 2,086 enemy soldiers.

For its extensive service, the men of the 65th Regiment were honored with two Presidential Unit Citations (Army and Navy), one Meritorious Unit Commendation (Army), one Navy Unit Commendation, two Republic of Korea Presidential Unit Citations, and the Bravery Gold Medal of Greece. Individual members of the unit were awarded nine Distinguished Service Crosses, some 250 Silver Stars, and more than 500 Bronze Stars for valor during their three years of fighting. According to military records, approximately 745 were killed and about 2,320 wounded.

General William W. Harris, in an account of the 65th Regiment, wrote, "No ethnic group has greater pride in itself and its heritage than the Puerto

Rican people. Nor have I encountered any that can be more dedicated and zealous in its support of the democratic principles for which the United States stands. Many Puerto Ricans have fought to the death to uphold them."

Other Hispanics in the Korean War

A number of Hispanics who fought during the Korean War went on to successful military careers. Among them was U.S. Air Force Captain Manuel J. Fernandez Jr., a fighter ace of the 334th Squadron, 4th Fighter-Interceptor Wing, who flew 125 combat missions over Korea.

Capt. Fernandez shot down 14 MiG-15 fighter aircraft and shared one additional kill. He was awarded a Distinguished Flying Cross and a Silver Star during his tour of duty. Fernandez remained in the Air Force after the Korean War, and eventually retired with the rank of colonel.

Richard E. Cavazos received a battlefield commission as an Army second lieutenant in 1951, and retired 33 years later as a four-star general. Cavazos was a decorated platoon and company commander in the Korean War, and served as a battalion commander in the Vietnam War.

Salvador E. Felices, a Puerto Rican who won a presidential appointment to the U.S. Military Academy at West Point, N.Y., in 1943, transferred to the Air Force when it was established in 1947. During the Korean War, he served as combat operations officer for the 98th Bomber Wing, flying 19 combat missions in B-29s over Korea in 1953.

The Vietnam War

Approximately 100,000 Hispanics served in America's armed forces during the country's 10-year involvement in the Vietnam War. Although military records are not definitive, it is believed that as many as 10,000 Hispanics lost their lives on the battlefield, or about 15 percent of the 48,000 war's casualties. About 30,000 were wounded. The records related to Latino soldiers who served, died, or were wounded in Vietnam are unclear because the U.S. military did not separate Hispanics by ethnicity throughout much of the war – Hispanics often were counted as Caucasians. Some military historians and research organizations of the Vietnam War claim that the Latino losses were as high as 25 percent.

Of the 239 Medals of Honor awarded during the Vietnam War, 13 were earned by Latinos. Nine of the 13 received their Medal of Honor posthumously. One of the most notable recipients was Special Forces Master Sgt. Roy P. Benavidez, a Mexican American native of El Campo, Texas. Taking charge of the rescue of a downed Special Forces team in May 1968, Benavidez, although seriously wounded during the operation, single-handedly saved the lives of eight men. During the rescue operation, Benavidez was wounded in the face, head, abdomen, back, and right leg. At one point, according to accounts, he was believed to be dead. In September 2000, the U.S. Navy honored Benavidez by naming a naval vessel in his honor.

The Gulf War

Out the 425,000 who served during the first Gulf War in 1991, about 25,000 were Hispanics. There were 26 Latinos who lost their lives in this conflict. Two high-ranking Hispanic officers of the U.S. Marine Corps played instrumental roles during the Desert Shield/Desert Storm war. Brigadier General Michael J. Aguilar served as the executive officer of Marine Aircraft Group 16 that supported the air and ground initiatives that contributed to the efforts to free Kuwait after it was invaded by Iraqi forces.

Brigadier General Christopher Cortez, who at one point in his career was head of the Strategy and Plans Division at the Pentagon, was also involved in Operation Desert Shield/Desert Storm, serving as a general in the Marine Corps.

The Iraq War

In July 2003, Lt. General Ricardo S. Sanchez was made the commanding officer and placed in charge of 130,000 American and 30,000 Allied troops from 34 coalition countries during the Iraq War. A three-star general, Sanchez was the highest ranking Hispanic in the U.S. Army, and the ninth Hispanic general in the Army's history. A native of Rio Grande City in South Texas, Sanchez grew up in poverty with his single mother, and rose to the top of his field by educating himself and working his way up the military ranks in a career that spanned 31 years. Sanchez served a year as a commanding general of his forces in Iraq before relinquishing his command over alleged abuses of Iraqi prisoners at Abu Ghraib prison near Baghdad. The highlight of his command was the capture of Iraqi dictator Saddam Hussein in December 2003 without a single shot being fired.

CHAPTER FOUR

At $1.33 Million Per Minute, America Cares

Consider this: In 2004, America's estimated 40 million Latinos will spend about $1.33 million per minute – that translates to $80 million per hour, $1.9 billion per day, or $700 billion per year. On an individual basis, it means that every Hispanic man, woman, and child spends on average $47.50 every day of the year.

On a more global scale, if Hispanics were a country unto themselves, their spending would place them in the No. 9 position, just below Canada and ahead of Spain and Mexico, according to the World Bank Group's 2002 worldwide ranking of nations' Gross Domestic Product (GDP).

The GDPs of Canada, Spain, and Mexico were $714 billion, $653 billion and $637 billion, respectively. With a population of 31 million and a national economy that is relatively comparable to the United States, Canada's position at No. 8 is not surprising. Spain's population of about 41 million most closely compares to America's Hispanic population numbers. But while it maintains a prominent position within the European Union, its economy has remained relatively static over the last six years.

Mexico, on the other hand, is a country of more than 100 million people, the largest Spanish-speaking country in the world. Its population is 2 times greater than America's Hispanic population, but its annual gross national income still lags $50 billion behind U.S. Latino spending.

Furthermore, researchers are projecting that by 2008, U.S. Hispanics' purchasing strength will bulk up to about $1 trillion per year. Those 60 seconds of Latino spending suddenly turn into $1.9 million, a spike of almost 43 percent in just four years. The colossal transformation of this market has been nothing short of phenomenal, especially since the $1 trillion projection is more than 4 times what Latinos spent in 1990, when their purchasing capabilities totaled only $222 billion. That represents a growth rate of 457 percent in an 18-year span, according to research done by the Selig Center for Economic Development at the University of Georgia.

The Selig Center, which was among the first research groups to predict spending would reach $1 trillion, also reported that the annual growth rate of Hispanic spending during the 18-year period is clocking in at an eye-popping compounded annual rate of 8.8 percent. By comparison, the rate of annual growth for non-Hispanics during the same period tracked at only 4.9 percent, about half as fast.

Even if one were to take a conservative approach by reducing the annual growth rate to a compound annual rate of 6.6 percent, projections to the year 2025 show that the overall purchasing strength of Hispanics would more than triple to $3.1 trillion per year. That figure would rank U.S. Hispanics above the GDP of every nation in the world except three: the U.S., Japan, and China, all global economic superpowers.

Is it any wonder that this segment of the U.S. population is suddenly turning heads? The good news is that U.S. Hispanics are not a country unto themselves, nor is there any credibility to the notion of Hispanics breaking off from America, as some have suggested. Hispanics aren't going anywhere. They are here to stay, and their world-class buying power has made them not only viable citizens but also extremely attractive consumers. Why else would hundreds of companies in corporate America – not to mention almost 2 million Latino-owned businesses – be scrambling to figure out how to capitalize on the unprecedented growth of an ethnic group that, more often than not, has been raked for its illegal immigration, its lack of education, or because it persists in clinging to its native Spanish tongue?

Social and political issues aside, it is impossible to ignore the impact of $700 billion in annual spending. It is occurring despite the fact that one in four working-age employed Hispanics earn less than $15,000 per year, or that Latinos represent one quarter of the American population who live below the poverty line.

It seems that the critical mass of the Hispanic community and retail consumerism have forged a strong partnership. It is a union yielding economic results that shows few signs of slowing down anytime soon. Especially given the U.S. census projection that the Latino population will grow from 40 million in 2004 to almost 60 million in 2020, to as high as 100 million in 2050, when Hispanics will represent 25 percent of the United States population.

Taking a theoretical page from the Selig Center projections, based on Hispanic spending reaching the $1 trillion plateau in 2008, a modest 5 percent annual compound rate to the year 2050 would push Hispanics' economic muscle to almost $14 trillion a year – a staggering number when you consider that the entire GDP for the United States in 2004 is between $10.5 trillion and $11 trillion.

Statisticians will warn against trying to accurately project that far into the future given all of the unknown factors that can affect the equation over a 42-year span. But if the U.S. Census Bureau is comfortable publishing population projections to 2050, there must be folks who have scribbled a few back-of-the-envelope economic forecasts. For example, how much revenue could be generated by capturing just 1/1000th of one percent of $1 trillion? The answer: $10 million.

It would be entrepreneurial ignorance – if not totally un-American – to neglect a projected $1 trillion-a-year market. The math is overwhelmingly attractive. Especially when market research shows how brand-loyal these particular customers are, how trusting they are of advertising messages –

particularly when they are delivered in Spanish – and how they are still evolving as consumers.

It's not as though this economic surge occurred overnight, although to some statisticians it may seem that way. Jeff Humphreys, director of the Selig Center, said up until 2001 most of the calls his group fielded were to answer questions regarding the demographics related to the African American market. "After 2001, after the new data was released from the 2000 U.S. census, the preponderance of calls were and have been about Hispanics," Humphreys said. It has been nothing short of "a wake-up call for corporate America," he said.

As far back as 30 years, demographers, social scientists, politicians, and journalists – mostly Hispanic – were touting the potential strength of America's Latino community. The catch phrase in those days was, "The numbers. Look at numbers." This was in the 1970s, when the U.S. Hispanic population numbered between 10 and 15 million.

The message from Latino leaders at that time focused mostly on the potential of Latinos on all fronts, but primarily in politics, education, immigration (mostly the undocumented) and, on occasion, economics. Beginning with the 1970s, every decade was trumpeted as the "Decade of the Hispanic." Every year was trumpeted as "The Year of the Latino," depending on who was holding the trumpet.

But in those days, the nation was preoccupied with other world events – the Vietnam War, the fall of President Richard Nixon, the 44 Americans taken hostage in Iran, the rise of President Ronald Reagan, the tearing down of the Berlin Wall, and the end of the Cold War. In those days, when media coverage touched on the civil rights movement, it was mostly in terms of black versus white. Latinos were an afterthought, passive participants in a loose-knit political alliance with blacks.

Even as we measure the impact of Latinos as a whole, there are serious social issues that must be addressed. Lofty consumer spending figures and the breathless media coverage they generated did nothing to mitigate Hispanics' other challenges – continued struggles with education and employment, excessive poverty, unacceptable teenage pregnancy rates, inordinate numbers of Latino families without health insurance, and barriers to homeownership.

It is a curious thing, though – coming at a time when Hispanics are the fastest growing and largest minority group in the U.S. – that there are few, if any, chants from Latino leaders saying this period of unprecedented growth represents yet another "Decade of the Hispanic." There has been relatively little chest-thumping on the subject, which is probably just as well since the overall numbers are a mixed bag of good news and bad.

"Certainly, the U.S. Hispanic market can be characterized as being in a state of dynamic flux, especially during the last 25 years," said Jesus Chavarria, publisher of *Hispanic Business*, which has chronicled Hispanic economic development. "This market's growth has been dramatic – fueled by demographic expansion as well as by rising demand and opportunity in U.S. labor and entrepreneurial markets."

But at the end of the day, what do the numbers really mean? What will purchasing power bring to Hispanics? Will they be discriminating consumers? Will they realize they can show brand loyalty with their dollars, thereby having a powerful impact on whether a company flourishes? Will they realize the dollars they put in corporate America's cash registers can result in higher Hispanic employment rates, increased economic development within the community, the development of better schools, or improved opportunities for homeownership?

Some Latino leaders believe the economic wave of purchasing power may represent the ultimate leverage Hispanics hold in American society now and in the years ahead. Perhaps. But one thing is for sure. The "anecdotal simplifications" associated with this market are a thing of the past, said Chavarria. The abundance of empirical data on Hispanics – much of it from the U.S. Census Bureau – is driving business decisions as never before. A host of market research firms are pumping out quantitative evidence showing that the Hispanic market is the place to be.

The numbers didn't support such a notion in the early days, when marketers tried to sell top management on the business case for diversity. Their reasoning was usually short on probabilities and long on the moral need to do the right thing. Both viewpoints are correct, of course, but nothing motivates corporate America like a profitable bottom line.

What's driving this potentially lucrative market? Why is it happening at such a blistering pace? And what does this kind of economic muscle translate into when equated with the continuing challenges Hispanics face? Let us further acquaint you with this hot ethnic market.

The Population

It is highly unlikely that any feature story about Hispanics would not include one of the following phrases embedded somewhere in the story:
"The fastest growing demographic group in the United States..."
"The largest minority group in the country..."
"Hispanics have overtaken blacks as the largest ethnic segment in the U.S...."
"Hispanics have had unprecedented population growth since 1970..."
"Large numbers of Latin American immigrants (legal and otherwise) and a high fertility rate have caused this growth..."
"The percentage of Latinos will continue rising at an unprecedented rate through the first 50 years of the century..."
"By 2050, Hispanics will account for 25 percent of America's population with more than 100 million..."
"Almost half of all Latinos live in just two states, California and Texas..."

To which we say: *"¿Y que?"* "So what?" The indisputable fact is the Latino population growth is unprecedented. The story behind these numbers will influence social issues for decades to come. "As it continues to grow, the composition of the Hispanic population is undergoing a fundamental change: Births in the United States are outpacing immigration as the key source of growth," according to a 2003 study by the Pew Hispanic Center, a research group located in Washington D.C. that specializes in Hispanic demographic issues. "Over the next 20 years this will produce an important shift in the makeup of the Hispanic population with second-generation Latinos – the U.S.-born children of immigrants – emerging as the largest component of that population."

The Latino population stands at approximately 40 million in 2004, or 13.7 percent of the total U.S. population, according to demographers. But that figure does not include another 6 to 8 million illegal Latino immigrants, nor does it include an estimated 4 million on the island of Puerto Rico, a U.S. territory with very close ties to Puerto Ricans in the U.S., primarily in New York and Florida. Altogether, the number of Hispanics in all three categories pushes the overall total to roughly 50 to 52 million.

Demographers estimate that 350,000 to 400,000 illegal immigrants (mostly Mexican) are coming into the United States each year. And if, as the Pew report predicts, births outpace immigration, these two categories alone could push the population figures up by about 800,000 per year. The table below projects Hispanics' rate of population growth into 2050.

Hispanic Population Growth Rate: 1970-2050

	Pop. (Millions)	Pop. Growth	% Growth	U.S. Pop.	% Hisp.
1970	9.6	—	—	203.2	4.7
1980	14.6	5.4	52.1	226.1	6.5
1990	22.5	7.9	54.1	248.7	9.1
2000	35.6	13.1	58.2	282.1	12.6
2010	47.8	12.2	34.3	308.9	15.5
2020	59.8	12.0	25.1	335.8	17.8
2030	73.1	13.3	22.2	363.6	20.1
2040	87.6	14.5	19.8	392.0	22.3
2050	103.3	15.7	17.9	419.9	24.6

Source: U.S. Census Bureau

Projected Hispanic Population Growth: 2000-2050

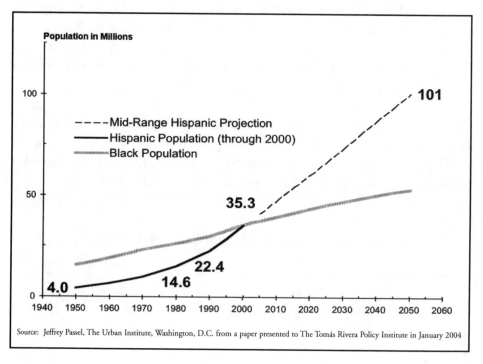

Source: Jeffrey Passel, The Urban Institute, Washington, D.C. from a paper presented to The Tomás Rivera Policy Institute in January 2004

One can see from the numbers that the Hispanic population almost quadrupled from 9.6 million in 1970, to 35.6 million in 2000, a phenomenal leap driven primarily by immigration and high fertility rates. The census bureau reported that in 1970, nine states had populations where Hispanics were the largest minority group in the state. In 2000, that number jumped to 23 states.

One also can see from the table that a hefty percentage of America's overall population growth will come from Latinos. For example, Hispanics will account for 45.5 percent of America's growth between 2000 and 2010. According to U.S. Census Bureau projections, those percentages will hover in the mid- to high-40 percent range until 2040, when they will surge above 50 percent.

Hispanics: Rich Diversity, Dense Enclaves

The diverse origins represented by the various Latino communities often present a challenge for marketers, policy makers, and service providers, among others. While Spanish may be a common bond, each subgroup boasts its own set of idiosyncrasies, whether it be the foods, music, or the traditions of their country of origin. To that end, there are dense enclaves that beget greater enclaves as wave after wave of incoming immigrants attempt to settle in among their own.

Hispanics are a rich, multicultural mix of nationalities: Mexican (almost 60 percent), Puerto Rican (8.6 percent), Cuban (3.7 percent), and Central and South American (16.3 percent). Nearly half live in centralized areas within a metropolitan city (45.6 percent). Another 45 percent live in the suburbs, but still within a metropolitan area, and about 8 percent live in non-metropolitan areas.

The Hispanic population story is one of dense clusters. More than three-quarters of all Latinos are concentrated in the West (43.5 percent), South (33 percent), and in a few large metropolitan regions in the Midwest (Chicago), and the Atlantic seaboard (New York and more recently Washington D.C.), according to HispanTelligence, a research arm of Hispanic Business magazine. Two states, California, with 11 million, and Texas with 6.7 million, represent almost half of all Hispanics in the nation. Five more states have populations of 1 million or more: New York (2.9 million), Florida (2.7 million), Illinois (1.5 million), Arizona (1.3 million,) and New Jersey (1.1 million).

Many believe that the city of Los Angeles is home to the largest Latino population. That title actually goes to New York, which has approximately 2.2 million Hispanic residents, the majority of whom are Puerto Rican. Los Angeles County and the greater Los Angeles area including Orange County and the Inland Empire, however, constitute the largest concentration of Hispanics of any area in the United States – it is home to more than 6.5 million Latinos. Miami-Dade, Harris (Houston), and Cook (Chicago) counties also have Hispanic populations of more than a million.

Nine States with Largest Latino Populations: 1960–2000

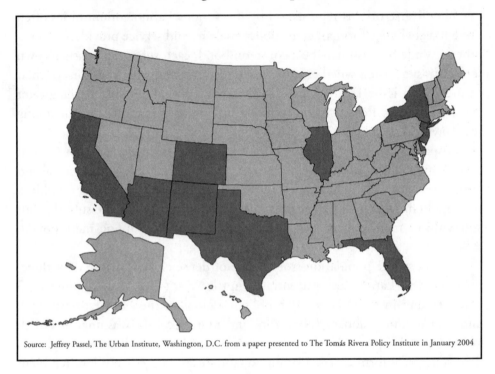

Source: Jeffrey Passel, The Urban Institute, Washington, D.C. from a paper presented to The Tomás Rivera Policy Institute in January 2004

What is interesting to note is that Latinos are beginning to settle in states that are not traditional destinations. For example, the Hispanic population increased dramatically between 1990 and 2000 in North Carolina (394 percent), Arkansas (337 percent), Georgia (300 percent), Tennessee (208 percent), Kentucky (173 percent), Minnesota (166 percent), and Nebraska (155 percent). Like all immigrants, Latinos are searching for their American Dream wherever opportunity takes them. There are jobs in these states – however modest the pay may be – and so they offer Latinos hope of building a better life. Modest-paying jobs in these nontraditional states include those in textile mills, poultry, and meatpacking industries – all tough work environments where these jobs are often left unfilled by area residents.

Hispanic communities have historically been populated regionally, by country of origin. This is still true. For example, Mexicans are heavily concentrated in the Southwest, primarily in California and Texas, where they make up 84 percent and 83 percent, respectively, of those states' Hispanic populations. Mexicans are also represented in large numbers in the Chicago area (estimated at more than a million), as well as Florida, Georgia, and New York.

There is also a strong Central American presence in California and Texas. California state officials report that outside the capital city of San Salvador, there are more Salvadorans living in the Golden State than any other place in Central America.

In New York, where 2.2 million Latinos constitute 27 percent of the city's total population, Puerto Ricans have long boasted the strongest Hispanic population totals. According to the census, an estimated 3.5 million Puerto Ricans live in the U.S. About a million live within the five boroughs of New York. Thousands more live outside the city in the suburbs of Long Island. An additional 340,000 Puerto Ricans reside across the Hudson River in New Jersey. The second largest group in New York is Dominican, which, in 2000, represented about 19 percent of all Hispanics in the area.

In Florida, Cubans represent the largest Latino group with 41 percent. There are, however, sizeable proportions of Puerto Ricans (18 percent), Mexicans (17 percent), and South Americans (13 percent).

Latinos have started migrating to non-traditional destinations like Georgia, the Carolinas, Arkansas, Tennessee, and Kentucky, which indicates they have become less risk averse in their pursuit of jobs and opportunities. It also shows a move away from states where traditionally they have found safety in numbers, but where they also encountered intense competition for jobs.

The Latino Family

There was a time when having large families was endemic to Latino life. This was especially true in Mexican households. If you grew up in the barrios of San Antonio or East Los Angeles, or even in a dusty, rural little town in the country in the 1950s or 60s, it was not unusual to see families with six or more children. You may still know some. In fact, they might even be your relatives or your neighbors.

Nobody picked on kids from those families, not when reinforcements were waiting just around the corner. When the family attended Sunday services, they filed into church in a long line and took up an entire pew. As the older siblings grew and produced their own offspring, the family took up yet another pew. Backyard gatherings were a major event, especially with the addition of other relatives who had their own large families in tow. Huge families crammed into tiny houses. Children slept three or four to a single bed, or on the floor.

If you grew up in South Texas, you saw Latino families pack the entire clan into cars and trucks, and hit the migrant farm worker route – some headed off to Florida to pick citrus, others north to the Midwest, to farms in Michigan and Wisconsin and then back through Colorado, timing the harvest work accordingly.

Everyone worked. If you could pull, pick, or carry crates of vegetables or fruit, you made your contribution. The bigger the family, the more revenue they earned. Education took a backseat. Some of the younger children might be sent to school for several weeks, only to be yanked out as the family moved on to the next harvest. It was, at best, a piecemeal education.

The nostalgia that some may feel for these large broods has given way to the financial reality of raising a family in today's economy. The costs associated with child rearing can be staggering. Saving for a child's education can virtually deplete a family's savings – if there is anything to deplete in the first place.

One could assume that given the high cost of living, large families – especially large Hispanic families – are a thing of the past. The size of the average American family has declined, from 3.1 to 2.6 persons during the last 30 years. Aside from financial demands, this can be attributed to a drop in fertility rates, changes in the living patterns of youth and fewer overall marriages, a higher median age for marriage, and increases in the divorce rate, according to the Population Resource Center (PRC), a Washington-based non-profit organization that provides educational programs based on demographic data.

But for Latinos, "big" remains in vogue. Even though the average Latino household nationally has 3.4 persons, of the 10.5 million total Latino households in the U.S., approximately one fourth had five or more people in the home. This was especially true of Mexican households, which accounted for more than 60 percent of all Latino households in the U.S. By comparison, less than 11 percent of all non-Hispanic white households were this large. Even more startling, there are 500,000 Hispanic households in the U.S. with seven or more people living at home, 82.6 percent of them Mexican.

It is apparent that the size of these households is the driving force behind Hispanic spending – a result of the massive and expensive process of feeding, clothing, housing, transporting, educating and, when possible, providing health care for a family of five or more.

These statistics are supported by the number of Hispanic births: One of every four babies born in the U.S. is to a Hispanic household. Higher fertility rates are a major source of population growth among minority groups, and Latinos have the highest fertility rate of any American minority, with the average woman giving birth to three children in her lifetime. The African American fertility rate is 2.2 lifetime births per woman, while non-Hispanic white women have the lowest fertility rate of 1.8.

On a median basis, Hispanics are more than 10 years younger than the general U.S. populace. In 2000, the median age for Hispanics was 26, versus 39 for white non-Hispanics. More than a third of Latinos are under the age of 18, compared with 22.8 percent of non-Hispanic whites. Relatively few Latinos are 65 and older (5.1 percent), compared with non-Hispanic whites (14.4 percent), according to the census.

One area of huge concern is the high level of teenage pregnancies. Hispanics have the highest teenage pregnancy rate of any racial or ethnic group in the U.S. Although the birth rate for Hispanic teens fell 12 percent between 1991 and 2000, the fertility rate of 94 births per 1,000 women age 15 to 19 was almost twice as high as the national average.

Hispanic Labor Force Projection: 2000-2050

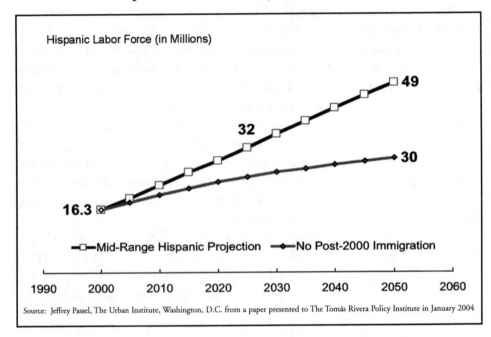

Hispanic Labor Force (in Millions)

49

32

30

16.3

—□—Mid-Range Hispanic Projection   —◆—No Post-2000 Immigration

1990   2000   2010   2020   2030   2040   2050   2060

Source: Jeffrey Passel, The Urban Institute, Washington, D.C. from a paper presented to The Tomás Rivera Policy Institute in January 2004

Labor

In 2004, more than 18 million Hispanics were working, a slightly higher proportion than either black or non-Hispanic men, according to HispanTelligence. In 2000, the PRC showed Hispanics had the highest labor force participation rates (68 percent for persons 16 and over) among all Americans. Hispanic women, however, had the lowest labor force participation rates at 57 percent, compared with 61 percent for non-Hispanic whites and 64 percent for black women.

The strength of the Latino work force will continue to rise in the coming decades and could represent a form of political leverage for Latinos. In 2004, one out of eight workers were Latino; in 2020 it will be one in six; by 2050 it will be one in four. Hispanics accounted for nearly a third of the increases in the U.S. labor force in the last 20 years, according to HispanTelligence. The Hispanic share of the U.S. labor force more than doubled to 12.4 percent between 1982 and 2002.

In 2002, Hispanics were twice as likely as non-Hispanic whites to work in service occupations, and as operators and laborers, according to the census. Conversely, only one in seven Hispanics were in managerial or professional occupations, a rate 2 times lower when compared with non-Hispanic whites.

Income & Earning Power

Among full-time, year-round workers in 2002, about a quarter of all Hispanics earned $35,000 or more, half the rate of non-Hispanic whites, according to the census. The median household income for Hispanics for a three-year average from 1998 to 2000 was $31,703, more than the $28,679 for blacks, but significantly less than the $45,514 earned by non-Hispanic whites, according to PRC.

On the down side, however, about 20 percent of Hispanics live in poverty (below $16,300), compared with about 8 percent of non-Hispanic whites. Hispanics represented 13.7 percent of the total population but constituted one fourth of the nation's population living in poverty. In addition, Hispanic children below the age of 18 are much more likely than non-Hispanic white children to be living in poverty. While Hispanic children represent about 18 percent of all children in the U.S., they represent 30.4 percent of all children in poverty, according to the census.

Despite high levels of poverty, a considerable segment of the Hispanic community has assimilated into American culture, and has begun transitioning toward middle-class affluence. Much of their ambition and drive has been propelled by improved educational gains and a sheer will to succeed.

The emergence of this middle class – as well as those who moved into the loftier income brackets – is primarily responsible for the bulk of the estimated $700 billion in annual purchasing power. There are indications that the momentum of this transformation will continue to grow based on the demographic trends of the last 20 years. In its study on the "Hispanic

Consumer in Transition," HispanTelligence outlined a number of factors that, in large measure, affirmed the velocity at which Latino purchasing power will expand, hitting the $1 trillion per year mark in the next four to five years.

The mean income of Hispanic households increased more than 37 percent, to $44,383 from 1970 to 2001, while the number of households earning more than $35,000 surged from 35.7 percent to 48.2 percent during the same period. Further, the percentage of Latino households earning more than $100,000 increased almost five-fold, representing about 735,000 Latino households nationwide.

About half of Latinos' net worth is concentrated in homeownership, compared to 33 percent among the general U.S. population, a clear indicator that Hispanics have not yet diversified their investment portfolios. What's more damning is that the level of homeownership among all Hispanics remained essentially static during the 20-year period from 1980 to 2000. During that span, homeownership inched up a scant 2.3 percentage points from 43.4 to 45.7 percent, according to HispanTelligence.

The aggregated net worth of the Hispanic population was at $534 billion in 2000, a hefty 31.2 percent jump from two years before. Still, that figure represented less than 3 percent of the total U.S. population's net worth.

Language

No issue has stirred the American public's emotions more than Latinos' ability to accept, learn, and use the English language. The controversy has sparked passionate debates and fits of righteous indignation in every camp.

The English-only advocates argue that the use of anything else is un-American, costly, and threatens "the whole notion of a melting pot culture." Ironically, the chairman of U.S. English, Inc., the nation's largest English-only organization with 1.7 million members, is Mauro Mujica, a Chilean immigrant. According to the group's website, "the high, uncontrolled rate of immigration to the U.S. is rapidly changing the face of our great country. From culture to politics, the way we function as a society is under stress."

Spanish-language proponents counter that English-only legislation could irreparably eclipse the Latino culture and heritage. Spanish is the primary means of communication among Latino families, they say, and it adds a layer of diversity to a country already rich in it.

James Crawford, a multilingual proponent and executive director of the National Association of Bilingual Educators, is the polar opposite of Mujica and a foe of the English-only crew. He is also white. "Despite its increasing diversity, the United States remains an underdeveloped country when it comes to language skills," Crawford wrote on his website. "Immigrants are importing other tongues at record rates. Yet the vast majority of native-born Americans remain stubbornly monolingual. Our ignorance of other languages and cultures handicaps us in dealing with the rest of the world. U.S. trade, diplomacy, and national security all suffer."

By Mujica's count, 27 states have adopted the idea of making English the official language. Crawford counted 22. Either way, it is clear Americans are divided.

Prior to the 2004 election, President George W. Bush and Democratic Sen. John Kerry launched multi-million dollar, Spanish-language media campaigns in an attempt to capture the Latino vote. In campaign speeches, both men patronize Latino voters with their Spanish phrases, and try to ingratiate themselves with a group they believe will play a pivotal role in several key states – despite that the vast majority of eligible Latino voters are primarily English-speaking citizens.

Still, what Latino immigrant would not be confounded by all of the hand-wringing over language in a country where the president and his political opponent are both speaking Spanish and asking for electoral support? What Spanish-dominant Hispanic would not be just a little bewildered by the angst among the English-only crowd, while corporate America daily unleashes a barrage of Spanish-language marketing campaigns via radio, television, newspapers, magazines, and the Internet? What Spanish-speaking Latino wouldn't be seduced by a Spanish-language media that includes an estimated 550 Spanish-language publications, 600 Spanish-language radio stations, 140 Spanish-language television stations, and who knows how many Internet sites, all operating within the largest English-speaking country in the world?

It isn't that Hispanics don't want to learn English – they do, and will eventually. Research shows strong signs that Latinos' ability to speak English improves dramatically with each generation. According to a Pew Hispanic Center study, "Although language proficiency in the first generation is overwhelmingly Spanish (62 percent) or bilingual (37 percent), the second generation is overwhelmingly proficient in English. The second generation is comprised of largely English speakers (21 percent) and English/Spanish bilingual speakers (74 percent), with only a small fraction that largely speaks Spanish (6 percent)."

Yet research also showed that while Hispanics may be embracing English, a large number are retaining and utilizing their Spanish. For this segment of the Hispanic population, which may number upward of 45 percent of the estimated 25 million Latino adults in America, being bilingual is a matter of personal practicality – it speaks to who they are, where they live, how cohesive their family situation is, and how and where they conduct business. It even mixes in a bit of cultural phenomena that Americans may not understand, acknowledge, or accept.

For example, there are countless Hispanics – some historians would say

---

Politics
Joseph Marion Hernandez, 1793-1857
Joseph Marion Hernandez was the first Latino U.S. congressman, serving as a representative from the Florida Territory and, later, as presiding officer of the Territorial House of Representatives. Although Hernandez lost his 1845 run for the U.S. Senate as a Whig, his service in Congress laid the path for future Latino legislators to follow, such as Jose Manuel Gallegos (1853-New Mexico); Romualdo Pacheco, the first Latino to hold a leadership position as chair of the Private Land Claims Committee (1877-California); Ladislas Lazaro (1913-Louisiana); and Ileana Ros-Lehtinen, the first Latina elected to the U.S. Congress (1989-Florida).

dating back to the early years of the 20th century who lived in households where family members moved from English to Spanish and back again, sometimes fluently, sometimes clumsily. They lived in homes where second- or third-generation Latino children navigated through linguistic crosswinds. They were immersed in learning English in American schools, but went home to parents and perhaps even grandparents who understood only a few English words and phrases. In many households, Latino children learned their Spanish through repetition, osmosis, or not at all – depending on the vigilance of the parents. In other cases, bilingual parents insisted the children speak only English at home as a way to get them Americanized as quickly as possible. Meanwhile, the parents communicated entirely in Spanish.

It was not unusual for a Latino child to conduct a conversation exclusively in English while a parent spoke entirely in Spanish, except for perhaps a few chopped up English words thrown in. But each managed to understand the other. Grandparents required a little more effort, with both grandchild and grandparent speaking in fractured English or Spanish phrases until they found a middle ground of communication. As they grew older together, they invented their own idioms, giving rise to what became "Spanglish" (Tex Mex in Texas), a bastardized form of English and Spanish melded together.

In retrospect, many Hispanic children, linguistically speaking, kept a foot in each world. The Pew study stated that "…adults who are English/Spanish bilingual readers are bilingual speakers. However, the converse is not necessarily true. Not all Hispanics who have bilingual speaking abilities are necessarily able to read both languages." The same can probably be said for writing in either language.

The current dilemma, at least for some Hispanics, is where to put their linguistic emphasis. Naturally, there is immense pressure to embrace English, the language of business, and the ultimate channel of communication. At the same time, there are immense social and cultural influences that entreat Latinos to retain Spanish. For many, Spanish represents their mother tongue. It also is the language of business in a multitude of Spanish-speaking communities, and the primary language of Latino family and friends.

The result: More Latinos are mastering English, but they are not giving up anything on the Spanish side of the language ledger. This is borne out in the research. HispanTelligence's studies found the number of U.S. Hispanics who speak both languages increased from 57 percent in 1995 to 63 percent in 2004, and is projected to rise to 67 percent by 2010. Further, the census reported that 78 percent of all U.S. Latinos speak Spanish (in varying degrees), including those who know English.

Given all of the media attention about Latino's growing purchasing power, their surge in population growth, and their geographic concentration in a handful of states, it becomes evident why marketing departments at numerous Fortune 100 companies are hard at work. With marketers, segmentation is the name of the game. And probably no factor has confounded companies more than trying to determine which of the two languages, English or Spanish, will be most effective. Some argue that the jury is still out on this issue because the Latino story continues to evolve. Others are already convinced.

People en Español magazine, with more than 4 million readers, in March 2003 released "Hispanic Opinion Tracker" (HOT), one of the most comprehensive and revealing studies of Hispanic consumers. The study was conducted with Cheskin Research, and consisted of more than 6,000, 30-minute bilingual telephone interviews (4,000 Hispanic, 2,000 non-Hispanic) from June through August of 2002.

"When you want to reach the vast majority of Hispanic Americans on a deeper level, to win their hearts as well as their attention, speak Spanish," the HOT study concluded. "Over 75 percent of the Hispanic population speaks Spanish at home. When looked at in terms of segmentation, 96 percent of Hispanic 'Dominants' speak Spanish most at home, 60 percent of 'Biculturals' speak Spanish most at home, and 9 percent of U.S. Dominants speak Spanish at home."

The HOT study further stated, "In a sea of American print and broadcast media, Hispanic Americans have to work a little harder to seek out Spanish TV, magazines and radio, but it is well worth it for the comfort and understanding they find there. Eighty-four percent of Hispanic dominant television viewing hours are in Spanish, 50 percent of bicultural television hours are in Spanish, and 9 percent of U.S. dominant television hours are in Spanish."

It is "clear that Hispanics do not adhere to old European immigration models," the study said. "Geography, technology, and the Spanish media keep all segments of the Hispanic American community connected to the Hispanic culture. And a constant flow of immigrants from Latin American countries renews and refreshes the Hispanic American community's cultural traditions."

Education: The Constant Challenge

Absolutely no issue ranks above education in terms of importance to Hispanics. It is the single-most critical concern for Latino parents, regardless of their national background. They know education is important because the issue has been hammered into them. Many also understand that the level of a person's education often correlates with success and earning power.

The most critical disconnect, some believe, comes from Hispanic parents who do not know how to navigate the American educational system to capitalize on opportunities that best serve their children. At the same time, American school systems are falling short in providing parents with sufficient assistance and direction in maneuvering through the maze of bureaucracy. More critically, in varying degrees, schools are not accommodating Hispanic parents' poor English-speaking skills, particularly among Spanish-dominant parents.

A Pew Hispanic Center report said that while Latino parents were "eager to engage the educational system and to take responsibility for ensuring their children's success," there were major concerns among Latino parents regarding the cultural divide between their children and teachers. "And yet Latinos are equally willing to assume some of the blame for not pushing their children hard enough," the report said.

The reality is that American school systems are faced with providing services to two sets of Hispanics – those who are U.S. born and whose parents (after two, three or four generations) are English-dominant and have assimilated into American life, versus foreign-born Latinos (parents and their offspring) who are Spanish-dominant, and who are thrust into school systems with little or no preparation. The steady stream of immigrant newcomers, estimated at 400,000 a year, will likely keep the foreign-born at one-third of the U.S. Hispanic population for several decades, according to Roberto Suro, director of the Pew Hispanic Center. Their presence means "Spanish is constantly refreshed, which is one of the key contrasts with what people think of as the melting pot," Suro said.

The challenge of educating these two different streams of Hispanic students will be made tougher as K-12 school systems and parents nationwide deal with sweeping changes associated with new federal requirements in the No Child Left Behind Act of 2001 (NCLB Act), which President George W. Bush embraced as the centerpiece of his education agenda.

Interestingly, while on one hand the Pew report said Latinos were willing to embrace the NCLB reforms more so than whites and blacks – Hispanics favored the use of standardized testing as a measure of achievement, for example – the report also noted that large numbers of Hispanics "are not aware of the fact that a major education reform has been enacted and lack information on key policy issues such as vouchers and charter schools." Again, another informational disconnect that has to be addressed.

In the meantime, the state of Hispanic students in America is a hodgepodge of good news (in relative terms) and bad news (in no uncertain terms). The U.S. Census Bureau reported that between 1970 and 2000 the percentage of Latino immigrants 25 and over who graduated from high school increased from 28 to 59 percent, while the number of U.S. born Hispanic graduates rose from 53 percent to 87 percent.

While the increases were significant, it also showed that a substantial number of immigrants were left behind educationally. The same was true at the college level where, during the same 30-year period, the number of Latino immigrants who attended at least two years of college doubled from 9 percent to 18 percent, while U.S.-born Hispanics doubled from 17 to 35 percent, according to census reports.

While it is not unusual for people to quote Hispanic dropout rates at anywhere between 30 to 40 percent, or even higher, there are two demographic sets of Hispanics and two distinct sets of dropout rates, each with its own story.

An updated Pew report on Hispanic dropouts in 2003 said the exaggerated dropout counts "include a great many immigrants who never set foot in a U.S. school. Counting only Latinos who dropped out after engaging the American education system yields a rate of about 15 percent among 16- to 19-year-olds. That is good news. The bad news is that this dropout rate is twice as high as the dropout rate for comparable non-Hispanic whites."

The 2003 Pew report stated that, because of the enormous growth in the number of Hispanic youth due to immigration and high birth rates, the number of Latino 16- to 19-year-old dropouts grew dramatically from 347,000 to 529,000 between 1990 and 2000. However, the dropout rate for native-born Latinos declined over that period from 15.2 percent to 14 percent.

Thirty-five percent of Latino youth were immigrants, the Pew report said, compared to less than 5 percent of non-Latino youth. Of the 529,000 16- to 19-year-old Latino high school dropouts in 2000, one out of three, or roughly 175,000, were immigrants who had little or no contact with U.S. schools. Even if you excluded that 175,000, there was still a staggering 354,000 U.S.-born Latino youths who dropped out.

Furthermore, Pew reported in January 2004 that the combined dropout rate for all Latino youth was at 21 percent, more than twice the national average at 10 percent. A lack of English-language ability was a prime characteristic of Latino dropouts. Almost 40 percent did not speak English well.

As immigrant flows continue and U.S.-Hispanic births remain on the upswing, is the same pattern to repeat itself between 2000 and 2010, or in the decade after that? Can Hispanics and America realistically accept the loss of roughly 350,000 to 400,000 high school dropouts per year? That's a loss of more than 3.5 million high school dropouts over just a 10-year span.

A student with a high school diploma will earn on average $7,800 more per year than one who did not graduate. Applying this amount to the 350,000 (low end) Latino high school dropouts per year, America is losing $2.73 billion in wages per year. Factor in an average of 30 percent federal tax assessment, not including state taxes, and the U.S. loses $819 million in federal taxes per year.

The same 350,000 high school dropouts, assuming they will work until age 60, using an annual 3 percent inflation adjustment (the average over the past 15 years), creates an estimated loss in earnings over the lifetime of these individuals of $11.5 trillion. How much will the federal government lose in taxes? Try $3.45 trillion.

Pew did report that even though Hispanic students who did not graduate from high school were somewhat less likely than comparable whites to pass a GED test, by the time they were 26-years-old, 43 percent passed the GED, compared with 50 percent of white dropouts. Subtract that 43 percent from the 3.5 million dropout figure above, and there still are 2 million Hispanics without a high school degree. Two million over a 10-year span – are 2 million reasons enough to motivate a community, a nation?

Does it get worse? Unfortunately, yes.

According to Pew statistics, among students who graduated from high school on time, Hispanics were much less qualified for college. A direct reflection on high school coursework, as well as academic achievement, the Pew Center said, only 53 percent of Hispanic high school graduates were at least "minimally qualified" for admission to a four-year college. In comparison, nearly 70 percent of white high school graduates were at least minimally prepared for college. At the upper end of achievement, Pew said 19 percent of Hispanic high school graduates were at least "highly qualified" for a four-year college, compared to 35 percent of whites.

In the fall of 2002, there were nearly 1.7 million Hispanic students enrolled in the nation's 4,100 degree-granting colleges and universities – 87 percent were undergraduates. Of this total, about 47 percent were in two-year community colleges and 53 percent were enrolled in four-year colleges and universities.

By age 26, Pew said, 18 percent of Hispanic high school graduates attained a bachelor's degree, less than half of the 38 percent among white students.

Health and Safety

America's Latino community is facing a serious health care crisis. Despite representing the fastest-growing population, and contributing both as workers and consumers to the nation's economy, Hispanics are twice as likely to be uninsured as the general population. It is estimated that almost 40 percent of all Hispanics under the age of 65 do not have insurance; three times the rate for the white adult population. During 2000, nearly one quarter of Hispanics with insurance and almost half of the uninsured had not seen a doctor, filled a prescription, or received recommended medical tests or treatment because of costs. What's more, half of Hispanics used a hospital or public clinic as their source of care, compared with 25 percent of whites and 40 percent of blacks.

Lower income accounted for some, but not all, of the disparity between Hispanic workers and other. Among families with incomes of less than $15,000, 45 percent of Hispanics were uninsured compared with 29 percent of whites and blacks. Among full-time Hispanic workers, 58 percent had coverage through their job, compared with 75 percent of blacks and 80 percent of whites. Those findings were reported in 2000 and 2001 in studies funded by the Commonwealth Fund Task Force on the Future of Health Insurance for Working Americans.

"This report sheds light on the multiple burdens faced by Hispanics, especially immigrants with low incomes, who contribute to our nation's economic success but face barriers to sharing in the results on an equal basis with other workers," said Karen Davis, president of the Commonwealth Fund, at the time the second report was released in June 2001.

"Recent rulings have pointed to the inequity of the 1996 restrictions on immigrants' access to Medicaid. Similarly, inadequacies in the private employer health insurance system negatively affect Hispanics' and other immigrants' ability to obtain coverage," Davis said.

The estimated Hispanic population in the United States in 2004 was about 40 million. It has been guesstimated that there are 6 to 8 million undocumented immigrants also working and residing in the U.S. Based on the Commonwealth reports, the total number of uninsured Latinos could be as high as 18.5 million. The number of uninsured Latino children under the age of 18 could be as high as 3 to 4 million.

The health care crisis has not lessened for Latinos since the second of the Commonwealth reports was released in 2001. If anything, the situation may have worsened.

A national report on America's uninsured, released in June 2004, claimed nearly 82 million people, or one third of the U.S. population younger than 65, was uninsured at some point over the previous two years, according to a story by the Associated Press (AP). The study, which was sponsored by the private group Families USA, indicated that Hispanics and blacks were disproportionately represented in low-paying jobs and in job sectors that were less likely to have health insurance benefits – agriculture and construction, for example.

The AP story reported that nearly 60 percent of Hispanics and 43 percent of blacks were uninsured, compared with whites at 23.5 percent. Therefore, the number of uninsured Hispanics could be as high as 27.6 million, representing one third of the nation's total insured, even though the Latino population only represents 13.7 percent of the total U.S. population.

The National Council of La Raza's Institute for Hispanic Health said Hispanics are particularly at risk because so many are Spanish-dominant – especially recent immigrant workers. Limited by language, many Hispanics encounter problems communicating health ailments to doctors. Language barriers also hinder patients' understanding of the doctor's instructions for prescription medicine and written information from the doctor's office. According to an NCLR study, nearly 50 percent of Spanish-speaking Hispanics reported having problems communicating with their physicians.

The NCLR figure on communication barriers was further substantiated in an investigative report released in January 2004 by the Association of Community Organizations for Reform Now (ACORN), the nation's largest community organization of low- and moderate-income families. ACORN had

Spanish-language testers call 70 hospitals and visit 15 hospitals throughout the nation to see if a Spanish-speaking staff person could be contacted, as required by law (Title VI of the Civil Rights Act of 1964). "In over 50 percent of the calls to the 70 hospitals tested and visits to the 15 hospitals, no Spanish speaker could be contacted," according to the ACORN report. "This shows how far the hospitals in America have to go in providing services to all Americans.

"Too often, people with limited English skills are forced to rely on untrained interpreters. Many times these are young family members. This can lead to embarrassment as privacy is violated. It can also lead to preventable illnesses and even deaths as medical terms are misunderstood and vital information fails to get through."

One of the study's most revealing findings came out of the Los Angeles area – which has the largest concentration of Hispanics (an estimated 4.2 million) than any other metropolitan center in the country. Spanish-speaking testers called 21 L.A.-area hospitals, and were unable to reach a Spanish-speaking hospital staffer in 44 percent of those calls.

In its own investigation during the spring of 2004, the Associated Press reported that U.S. jobs were claiming an immigrant victim a day in work-related accidents. "Though Mexicans often take the most hazardous jobs, they are more likely than others to be killed even when doing similarly risky work," according to the AP story. The investigation revealed that death rates were greatest in several Southern and Western states, where Mexican workers were four times more likely to die than the average U.S.-born worker.

"These accidental deaths are almost always preventable and often gruesome," the AP said. "Workers are impaled, shredded in machinery, buried alive. Some are 15 years old."

AP investigators talked to scores of workers, employers, and government officials, and analyzed years of federal safety and population statistics. Mexican death rates were rising even as the U.S. workplace was growing safer overall, the AP concluded.

In the mid-1990s, Mexicans were about 30 percent more likely to die than native-born workers. "Deaths among Mexicans in the United States increased faster than their population. As the number of Mexican workers grew by about half, from 4 million to 6 million, the number of deaths rose by about two-thirds, from 241 to 387. Deaths peaked at 420 in 2001."

The AP's investigation focused on 1996 through 2002, which provided the most recent set of worker death data from the U.S. Bureau of Labor Statistics. Those were years when the economic boom coaxed about 1 million Mexicans beyond the border states. During those years, the AP analysis showed, Mexicans were increasingly more likely to die on the job than U.S. workers of any race. Construction was the deadliest industry. Many of the deaths were the result of poor training, communication barriers, and workers' willingness to perform high-risk jobs no one else wanted to do.

Community Advocacy
Antonia Pantoja, 1922-2002
Recognized as one of the foremost political advocates for the Latino community, Antonia Pontoja was the founder of ASPIRA (which takes its name from the Spanish verb aspirar, "aspire"), a nationally-recognized nonprofit organization committed to the development of Puerto Rican/Latino community leadership. Prior to ASPIRA, her hard work, commitment to public service, and passion for social justice led her to earn a master's degree in social work at Columbia University, represent the Puerto Rican community as a member on the New York Commission on Intergroup Relations, establish the Puerto Rican Forum, and help implement the War on Poverty, the domestic policy plan of former President Lyndon B. Johnson. Her autobiography, Memoir of a Visionary: Antonia Pantoja, won the Presidential Medal of Freedom in 1996.

Immigration

Are Hispanic immigrants – particularly those here illegally – a financial benefit or an enormous expense? Do they really take jobs no one else wants?

Are they as hard-working as many claim, eager to settle for below-scale pay without complaint, even in the face of unsuitable working conditions? Or are they siphoning off millions of dollars worth of public assistance, including schooling, health care, and other government services? Critics argue that they persist in speaking Spanish. They keep to themselves. They don't weave themselves into the fabric of America society. With a record number of about 400,000 Latino immigrants coming into the U.S. each year, many Americans wonder if the flow will ever taper off.

Good questions. Are there answers? Yes, but probably none that will satisfy activists or critics on either side of the immigration issue. This is a controversy that, like it or not, has long legs. Always has, probably always will. And yet, strangely enough, it is a sad tell-tale slice of Americana – people with absolutely nothing in their pockets and very little on their backs, bedraggled folks who come here with hopes and dreams, only to turn around and begrudge the next wave of immigrants their own fortunes.

There is a part of America that looks nostalgically on immigration – huddled masses on transport ships passing by the Statue of Liberty, future patriots landing at Ellis Island, hardy Europeans making their way to the New World. Countless movie clips have captured this poignant moment. The Ellis Island Immigration Museum commemorates the arrival of an estimated 12 million people who passed through during the first half of the 20th century. Historians have chronicled how each ethnic group – be it Irish, Jew, Italian, Polish – experienced its own nasty form of discrimination and racism. But they all survived. America survived, as well. So what, then, makes Americans so uncomfortable about Hispanic immigration?

To be sure, the immigrant numbers (legal and otherwise) seem gargantuan when compared to the numbers that passed through Ellis Island. But the population of the United States during the first half of the 20th century was much smaller, ranging from 76 million in 1900 to 158 million in 1950 – an increase that no doubt was helped along by the 12 million immigrants who arrived during this period.

Demographers will say that the level of Hispanic immigration America has witnessed in the last 30 years represents only the rising crest of what will likely be a tsunami of population growth over the next five decades. Geographic proximity will provide much of the swell, particularly from Mexico, the largest feeder country. It will certainly bring with it a tsunami of controversy as well.

On one side, critics will lay in with claims that non-citizen immigrants cost America's health care system billions of dollars annually. Their argument will be a repeat of a 1997 report that said Medicaid expenditures for non-citizens were $8.1 billion, or about 7 percent of all Medicaid expenses. That same year, however, the National Academy of Sciences concluded that immigration provided $10 billion in net benefits to the American economy.

There will be those who say the immigration issue is divided by the haves and the have-nots. *American Demographics*, a magazine specializing in the examination of demographic trends, reported in 2000 that "lower-income, less-educated folks are more likely to say immigrants are a burden to the country and take jobs away from Americans than upper-income, better-educated people." The magazine quoted from a poll conducted by Princeton Survey Research and the Pew Center, which found that 46 percent of those making less than $20,000 per year considered immigrants a burden, compared with only 21 percent of those making more than $75,000 per year.

The magazine also reported that, according to a Gallup Poll, 54 percent of college graduates believed immigrants become productive citizens in the long run. Only 40 percent of those with a high school education agreed. According to the magazine, "Those with a lower income and less education generally feel more insecure economically and thus, may feel more threatened by job competition with immigrants than other groups."

Sometimes, though, it's simply a matter of perception. DiversityInc.com, an Internet service that examines minority issues, reported in August 2003 that, in a poll taken by the Market Segment Group, 82 percent of Latinos, 67 percent of African Americans, and 53 percent of whites believed most immigrants arrived in the United States illegally. "Poll after poll reveals that the American people do not typically draw clear distinctions between illegal and legal immigrants," said Peter Skerry, a governmental studies professor, who was quoted in the DiversityInc.com story. "However unfortunate from a civil-liberties point of view, this perspective is hardly irrational. Illegals are part of the (fabric) of American society."

What many people may not realize is the majority of immigrants are here legally. The census bureau estimated the number of illegal immigrants at about 7 million – other veteran demographers say the number is higher. There were actually 21.6 million legal immigrants in America in 2003, according to a DiversityInc.com report. Estimates by the U.S. Department of Homeland Security's Bureau of Citizenship and Immigration Services showed about 50 percent of the illegal immigrant population arrived in the country legally and simply overstayed their visas.

Labor shortages in the American job market, particularly in low- to middle-paying jobs, could create new opportunities for immigrants. According to an *American Demographics* analysis in November 2001, several trends will drive these shortages. The biggest factor will be the decline in U.S. births; the Baby Boom produced Generation X, which will, in turn, produce fewer future workers. As a result, by the end of this decade there will be a 12 percent decline in the 35- to 44-year-old age segment, and a 3 percent decline in the 30- to 34-year-old age group. Just as Baby Boomers are entering the stage of life where they will need more health care, there may not be enough workers to provide it. Unless there is another big jump in immigration, by 2010 there will be at least 5 million fewer workers age 30 to 44.

Compounding the loss of workers is that more of the Gen Xers in the 20- to 29-year-old age range are taking themselves out of the labor force to attend college or graduate school. The National Center for Education Statistics projected that by 2010 approximately 16.5 million will be college or university students, up 10 percent from 2001. Further, the U.S. Department of Labor's Bureau of Labor Statistics predicted that sometime during this decade a gap would emerge in which there would be at least 3 million more job openings than laborers to fill them.

These predictions suggest at least two possible responses: First, the specter of federal legislation permitting more immigration, perhaps including selected amnesty for those without a green card. In fact, President George W. Bush announced in January a plan to revamp the nation's immigration laws, and allow some 8 million illegal immigrants to obtain legal status as temporary workers.

The second prediction was that real inflation-adjusted wages for service workers would likely rise, luring a portion of the 28 million retirees back into the work force.

Another reason immigration could be beneficial in the years ahead is that the median age of immigrants is very young. Further, the birth rates of first-generation immigrant women tend to be higher than those born in the United States (3.1 versus 2.1). Consequently, while the population in most European countries is aging, potentially putting pensions at peril, America's immigrants, who have a higher labor-participation rate than non-immigrants, and who lower the average age of the non-retired work force, will help support programs such as Social Security.

In the meantime, the immigrant force continues to toil away, taking low-paying jobs, sometimes taking two jobs to stay ahead, setting aside money for its American dreams and, when possible, sending money home. The latter has been no small undertaking, and not without its own surprising results.

The Inter-American Development Bank (IADB) recently released a study showing that immigrants in the U.S. send a record $30 billion to their families and friends in Latin America. Remittances range from 50 to 80 percent of household income, depending on the country.

"Remittances have become a major source of capital for Latin America and the Caribbean, which last year received more than $38 billion from its expatriates around the world (about 75 percent of the money was sent from the United States)," the report said. "These flows not only outstripped all the overseas development aid to the region but also topped the foreign direct investment registered in 2003."

On average, Latino immigrants send money home once a month, typically in amounts ranging from $150 to $250 per transfer. The IADB said that, unlike previous surveys of remittance senders, it found a great number of people send money more than once a month, most likely a reflection of the fact that transfer fees have dropped by almost half in recent years.

The IADB report said recently arrived immigrants earning low wages were more likely to send money to their home countries than their more established counterparts. Still, a majority of respondents said they had been sending money home for more than five years. Immigrants in six states send more than $1 billion per state to Latin America; the top two in remittances were California with $9.6 billion, and New York with $3.56 billion.

The New Latinos

As the Hispanic population in America exploded in the last three decades, the composition of immigrant groups saw a major shift, particularly during the last 10 to 15 years. For decades, Mexicans, Puerto Ricans, and Cubans were responsible for most of the immigration into the United States. While Mexicans still accounted for two-thirds of all immigrant flow, census reports showed waves of "New Latinos" were arriving from the Caribbean and Central and South America, and from countries like the Dominican Republic, El Salvador, Guatemala, Colombia, Peru, and Ecuador.

According to the Lewis Mumford Center for Comparative Urban and Regional Research, which has focused on the New Latino movement, the number of immigrants in this category more than doubled, from 3 million in 1990 to 6 million in 2000.

According to the center, Puerto Ricans and Cubans are still the second and third largest Latino subgroups in the U.S., but there are now nearly as many Dominicans and Salvadorans as Cubans. Dominicans and Salvadorans constituted the largest of the New Latino groups, having doubled their population to more than 1.1 million between 1990 and 2000. It is likely that, given their fertility rates, these groups will outnumber Cubans in the next few years.

In profile, Dominicans stand out for their low income – their mean earnings fall below $8,000 a year, and more than a third live in poverty. Dominicans also have higher than average unemployment, and are the group most likely to receive public assistance.

The earning power of the major Central American groups (El Salvador, Guatemala, Honduras and Nicaragua) most closely resembles that of Puerto Ricans, but they are far less likely to fall below the poverty line. They are also three times less likely to receive public assistance than either Puerto Ricans or Dominicans (an overall average of 2.4 percent versus 7.3 percent and 8.2 percent respectively).

New Latinos from South America, on the other hand, immigrate to the U.S. with a stronger overall profile. Immigrants from Colombia, Ecuador, and Peru arrive as the most educated among all Hispanics, with 12.6 years of formal schooling. They have the highest earning average of any Latino group and, far and away, are at the lowest level of all Hispanic people living below the poverty line and receiving public assistance.

Top Five States for New Latinos

New York has attracted the most New Latinos, close to 1.4 million. About half were Dominicans, whose population jumped by almost 80 percent from 1990 to 2000. When combined with the immigrants from Central and South America, these New Latinos have overtaken Puerto Ricans as the primary source of Hispanic immigration. Interestingly, the number of Mexican immigrants in the state tripled to almost 275,000, serving notice of that group's growing mobility.

New Jersey reflected a similar picture to that of its New York neighbor, but on a much smaller scale. Like New York, Puerto Ricans represented about a third of the state's Latinos. But here, too, New Latino immigration for the first time outpaced Puerto Ricans numbers (more than 500,000 in 2000).

California drew almost as many New Latinos as New York (also close to 1.4 million). According to the Mumford work, the state's largest share of immigrants – over a million – were from Central America, including El Salvador, Guatemala, and Nicaragua.

Although Florida's Hispanic population was well distributed among many national-origin groups, Cubans were still the largest, with nearly 900,000 residents statewide. However, the Mumford analysis indicated that Cuban growth slowed during the 1990s, and that their number was nearly matched by New Latinos.

Growth Rate of Latino Population by State: 1990–2000

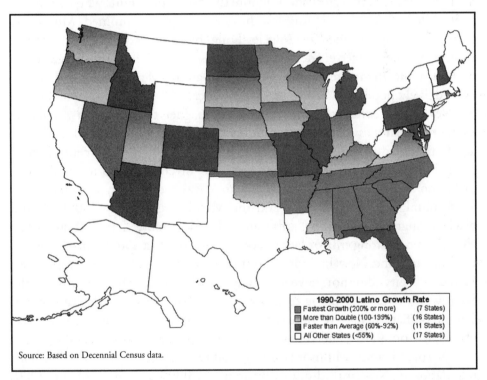

1990-2000 Latino Growth Rate
- ■ Fastest Growth (200% or more)   (7 States)
- ▨ More than Double (100-199%)   (16 States)
- ■ Faster than Average (60%-92%)   (11 States)
- □ All Other States (<55%)   (17 States)

Source: Based on Decennial Census data.

Texas had 400,000 New Latinos. The largest share comes from Central America, especially El Salvador. This population was barely noticeable statewide, however, because it was outnumbered by 6 million people of Mexican origin.

Metropolitan Enclaves

The Los Angeles metropolitan area claimed the largest foreign-born population with 3.4 million. More than 2 million were Latino, and of this figure, the vast number were Mexican. Asians made up a large portion of the rest. The 2 million were more than double the number of Latino immigrants in any other location. One cannot ignore the mass immigrants who live within a 50-mile radius of Los Angeles, however. If you combined Mumford's population tally for the Los Angeles-Long Beach metro area with Orange County and nearby Riverside-San Bernardino, the overall count surged to 6.5 million, more than three-quarters of whom are of Mexican origin. It is the most densely populated Latino area in America.

New York represented the other great magnet to immigrants. The Big Apple had nearly as many immigrants as Los Angeles (3.1 million), and grew at a faster rate during the 1990 to 2000 period (up about 40 percent). What's more, New York's immigrant growth was more diverse. Second to Los Angeles in Latino and Asian immigrants, New York was the primary destination for white immigrants from Europe and the Middle East (nearly 750,000), and black immigrants from the Caribbean and Africa (more than 500,000). The city boasted a strong mix of large Latino groups that included Puerto Ricans, Dominicans, and New Latinos (2.94 million in the greater New York area). While the city did not have as many Mexicans as other metros in the Southwest, it was still home to almost 300,000 residents of Mexican origin. On top of that, there were more than 700,000 Asians, including large numbers of people from China and India.

Of special note, Mumford's study pointed out, was that the U.S.-born population of New York dropped by about 80,000 between 1990 and 2000, while the number of foreign-born jumped by 850,000. "The number of white New York natives dropped even more, by nearly 450,000, and there were few new white immigrants. In this case the region would have lost population if not for growth in the number of black, Hispanic, and Asian immigrants."

Chicago, the primary destination point in the Midwest, had almost 1.5 million immigrant residents, placing it third in the nation. Chicago has long been a destination point for immigrants from Eastern Europe. The largest immigrant group, however, was represented by Latinos (mostly Mexican), who numbered about 700,000. The third largest group was Asians with 300,000.

Miami had more than 1.1 million immigrants. The vast majority (900,000) were Latinos, with much of the growth coming from South Americans, Salvadorans, and Nicaraguans, complementing the large Cuban population. Nearly 100,000 of these new immigrants were black, about equally from Haiti and the English-speaking Afro-Caribbean nations.

Houston and Dallas were both counted among the top 10 in number of immigrants. The Latino immigrant population more than doubled in the last decade. In addition to Mexicans, Houston became a major destination port for Salvadoran immigrants. Both metro areas were home to more than 100,000 Asian immigrants, who doubled their count in the last decade.

The nation's capital, Washington, DC. attracted a swell of new immigrants that was as racially diverse as that of New York, with nearly equal shares of Asians and Hispanics, and a significant minority of white and black immigrants.

Hispanics also have begun to make inroads into large and medium-sized metros in the Southeast and interior West — areas that were traditionally dominated by domestic migration, whites, and blacks, according to *American Demographics*. In a December 2000 article, the magazine reported that cities like Atlanta, Charlotte, Raleigh-Durham, Greensboro, Orlando, and West Palm Beach were Southern metros that showed high rates of Hispanic gains. In the West, the magazine pointed to new Hispanic frontiers, including Las Vegas, Portland, Salt Lake City, and Seattle. A number of Midwest areas also made the magazine's list, including Minneapolis-St. Paul and Kansas City. Four years later, all these cities continue to show strong growth.

CHAPTER FIVE

Hispanic Purchasing Power on the Rise

Somewhere the late farm labor activist Cesar Chavez must have been smiling. The founder of the United Farm Workers of America, who spent a great deal of his life battling on behalf of thousands of Mexican farm laborers for improved working conditions, union rights, and better wages, would have found a bit of irony in a press release that was circulated with little fanfare by Beringer Vineyards, the oldest winemaker in California's Napa Valley.

The 128-year-old wine producer was announcing the introduction of a Spanish bilingual label for its award-winning Beringer White Zinfandel. The use of Spanish on the Beringer label and on its point-of-sale promotions in retail outlets, the press release said, was indicative of the company's commitment to the growing Latino market.

"It's about time we in the wine industry recognize the importance of the U.S. Latino consumer. Forty percent of Latinos in the U.S. drink wine at least once a week," said Dan Leese, managing director of Beringer Blass Wine Estates. "By offering a multiple language label on our popular White Zinfandel, we are responding to a real consumer need."

Another Beringer representative chimed in with glowing praise. "I'm proud to say that the Latino community has been an essential part of Beringer Vineyards' success story since our founding in the late 1800s," said Cristina de la Presa Owens, a member of Beringer's winemaking team. "It seems very fitting that Beringer Vineyards is now offering a Spanish-language label on the country's top-selling bottled wine."

Very fitting indeed. Chavez, who for more than four decades tenaciously negotiated UFW union pacts with winemakers and growers in California, might have categorized Beringer's marketing strategy under the heading of "better late than never."

The struggle for Latino farm workers' labor rights was won on the backs of thousands of Mexicans who toiled in the vineyards and fruit and vegetable fields of California for companies like Beringer, Gallo, Schenley, DiGiorgio, and Giumarra, and scores of other growers. The toe-to-toe dealings between the UFW and the growers were legendary, at times violent and bloody, sometimes leading to worker killings.

In 1967, Chavez called for a nationwide boycott of all California table grapes. A 1975 Harris Poll estimated that about 17 million Americans boycotted grapes in support of Chavez and the UFW. While the UFW eventually triumphed, the grape boycotts of the late 1960s and early 70s still resonates among Latinos – there are those who, to this day, refuse to purchase grapes in reverence for what Chavez and the UFW achieved.

So when the granddaddy of all vineyard operations came out with its bilingual wine label, and its executives swooned about "the importance of the U.S. Latino consumer," well, it does make longtime Latino watchers wonder if there just might be some truth underneath all of the hype and hoopla over Hispanic purchasing power.

No doubt Chavez would have cherished the Beringer moment, irony and all. "It's smart marketing," said Marc Grossman, once a close aide of Chavez and today the UFW's director of communications.

Hispanics are beginning to cherish their own moments as well. They are suddenly hip and cool. Their foods are popular nationwide – there are even reports that salsa is outselling ketchup. Breakfast burritos have become a morning staple of fast-food chains. Tortillas are the new bread. Not to be left in the dust by the popularity of low-carbohydrate diets, Mission Foods, the world's largest tortilla producer, this year introduced a new line of low-carbohydrate products that have substantially fewer "net" carbohydrates, and are higher in protein than regular tortillas. AC Nielsen reported that sales of breads, bagels, rice, pastas, and cookies are all down, while corn tortillas are up 10 percent and flour tortillas up 4 percent.

For the fourth year in a row, Jackson and Perkins, the world's largest grower of roses, is featuring a rose named Our Lady of Guadalupe, a popular flower named after the patron saint of Mexico. A percentage of the proceeds are donated to Hispanic college funds.

Salsa, meringue, and Tex-Mex music have people of all backgrounds grinding around the dance floor. Cinco de Mayo has become an unofficial holiday, much like St. Patrick's Day. According to ParentsPlace.com, the most popular boy's baby name in Texas in 2002 was Jose. The highest paid and presumably best player in major league baseball, Alex Rodriguez – A-Rod, as he is known in baseball circles – has taken center stage on the grandest stage of all, playing for the New York Yankees, and reaping the rewards of a contract totaling more than $250 million over 10 years. Nick Jr.'s *Dora the Explorer*, the highest-rated pre-school show on commercial television among kids aged 2 to 5, features the cartoon world's first Hispanic heroine. New lines of *Dora* toys are already in stores. In an attempt at crossover appeal, Mattel recently introduced Christina Aguilera and Shakira look-alike dolls to attract Hispanic teens. Hershey Foods hired Mexican singer and soap opera star Thalia Fodi for its Spanish-language ads. Marvel Comics debuted *Amazing Fantasy*, about Anya Corazon, a school girl from Brooklyn with spider-like powers. The first edition sold out in two weeks.

These are heady days for Hispanics. For decades, Latinos have been like the student at the rear of the class, waving his arm frantically but failing to get the teacher's attention. The student is growing up and the teacher can't help but notice. America cannot help but notice, either.

Years from now Latino historians may well look back on the year 2000 as a watershed. Hispanics may look back on the development of the Hispanic market in terms of "Before the U.S. Census 2000" and "After the U.S. Census 2000."

"Before 2000" were the anecdotal years, when corporate America's legions of marketers and business analysts spoke about the potential of the Hispanic market in halting qualitative terms. Hispanics were just another minority that companies were obligated to include in their business case arguments for diversity.

The 2000 census changed everything. Its reams of quantitative data legitimized and validated Hispanic population figures, household characteristics, purchasing habits, generational differences among immigrants from Mexico and South and Central America, the rapid growth of Hispanic-owned businesses, the changing role of Latinas, the impending influence of Hispanic youth, the cultural significance of the Spanish language, and on and on and on.

Lest anyone think the data magically appeared one day, they should know that countless demographers deciphered the Latino story long before the U.S. Census Bureau. But the story and the data behind it never achieved national prominence until the census bureau put its official government stamp on its findings.

Suddenly the data had authority, legitimacy. Hispanics had never before been seen as anything other than a quiet, unassuming group of cheery, festive people who, save the few Chavez's of the world, made little economic or political noise. Now there was no denying its phenomenal growth. Overnight, or so it seemed, people were talking about 40 million people spending $700 billion a year – a population figure projected to grow to almost 70 million by 2025, with purchasing power approaching $2.5 trillion.

Today, the rush is on. Companies large and small are attempting to capitalize on the purchasing patterns of an ethnic group that in 2000 surpassed blacks in population numbers, and by 2009 will outdistance them in purchasing power. That little boy waving his hand at the back of the class

Hispanic Purchasing Power and
Overall Percent of National Purchasing

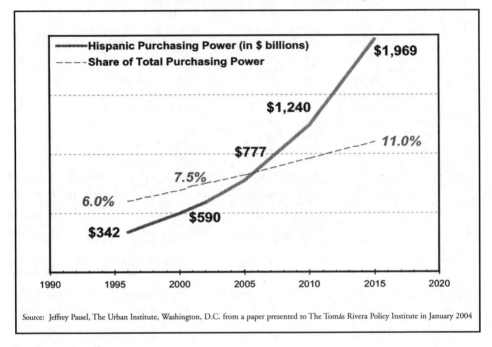

Source: Jeffrey Passel, The Urban Institute, Washington, D.C. from a paper presented to The Tomás Rivera Policy Institute in January 2004

finally took a front row seat.

Beringer Vineyards has not been alone in its praise of the Hispanic consumer. In spite of a sordid history with the UFW, California growers and wineries are coming to the realization that their fields are being harvested by Latino workers, and their products are being purchased by Latino customers in a state where Latinos represent one in three of all consumers. In the next 20 years that ratio will move toward one in two – half. By 2050, could Latinos possibly represent a majority in California? It's not so far-fetched.

In the meantime, corporate marketing departments nationwide are throwing teams of analysts and researchers at the Hispanic market, each in search of a viable market niche. Non-participation in this growing demographic is not an option for these companies – not when there's $700 billion at stake this year and trillions of dollars on the horizon.

There will be a parade of countless other companies issuing press releases and holding press conferences, paying homage to the Latino consumer. They will talk about how Latinos are the fastest growing minority in the United States, and how much their culture has contributed to the diverse fabric of America. Underneath their rhetoric and platitudes will be the real motive – money. The number of Hispanic dollars being spent, where it's spent, how it's spent, how often, and how loyally. It will be about margins and bottom lines and what percentage of $700 billion they can capture.

"I think what the Hispanic community is enjoying now is the recognition for its economic power," said Felipe Korzenny, a co-founder of Cheskin Research and now a professor of Hispanic marketing at Florida State University. "I think that is an important part of the self-concept of Hispanics these days, because usually we have been treated as second-class citizens, particularly in the West and Southwest. When you are beginning to be valued because you have economic power, it changes the way people look at you, and it changes everything. And actually, I think it is a good thing."

It is almost impossible to accurately discern how many in the nation's Latino community are actually aware of their economic power, or whether it would matter to them even if they did know. For Hispanics who traffic in financials, that kind of a figure might bring a raised brow and a spark of cultural pride. For the struggling Latino laborer, who is trying to hold down jobs and put food on the table, it's just another meaningless factoid.

But it does have meaning, Korzenny pointed out. It means Hispanics are valuable consumers. And that, all by itself, is a comfort food for which Latinos don't have to pay.

It also means companies that want the Hispanic dollar will have to think twice about the level of customer service they offer. Older Latinos haven't forgotten a time, not so long ago, when they shuffled into stores, hats in hand, afraid to make eye contact with store clerks who eyed them suspiciously as they browsed the shelves. Today, Hispanics should be walking into department stores with a bounce in their step, expecting to be greeted with a smile: "May

I help you? Please?" If it doesn't happen, they should learn how to vote with their feet and take their business elsewhere – just as any American would.

Some say the impending shift has shaken the marketing industry to its foundation. That remains to be seen. What is changing is that American companies are incorporating multicultural marketing schemes into core business strategies. It is an approach that encompasses Hispanics, African Americans, Asian Americans, and Native Americans, all of whom will account for more than $2.5 trillion in spending by the year 2010. But it goes even deeper than that. Within each ethnic group there are distinct subgroups, each requiring its own approach, cultural segmentation, medium, and even its own language. The situation has many a marketer walking on egg shells, trying to learn the do's and don'ts of this multi-faceted, multi-layered market.

Hispanics comprise more than 20 subgroups, each with its own colloquial Spanish, foods, customs, values, and cultural idiosyncrasies. Hispanics are not monolithic – they can be of any race, each of them proud of their individuality. The marketer who equates a Puerto Rican with a Mexican, a Mexican with a Cuban, a Cuban with a Dominican, is in for a rough ride.

Language will be an enormous factor. Should the marketing campaign be in English or Spanish, or a bilingual blend of both? The data clearly show certain developmental phases which foreign-born, first-generation immigrants go through as they settle into American society, and begin to grapple with its customs and language. These stages will be very different than those of their American-born children, or from the second, third, and fourth generations. Marketing not only becomes about product, then, but also about where along the Hispanic generational continuum the company focuses its campaign.

Correctly choosing the best channel of communication will be another difficult and potentially bewildering task, particularly in a media world where fragmentation rules. There are hundreds of cable TV stations, radio stations, magazines, newspapers, and upward of 60 million Internet websites in the U.S. alone – the vast majority of which use English. The marketer who wants to send a message in Spanish will have to choose from more than 140 Spanish-language television stations, 600 Spanish-language radio stations, and more than 500 Spanish-language magazines, newspapers, and websites.

"For Hispanics, color is not as big a deal as it is with the blacks because Hispanics can be white, can be black and can be yellow. Hispanics come in all colors," said Korzenny. "It is not a race. It is a culture. When you see your culture reflected, your sense of humor reflected, when you see a little bit of your language, no matter what, your language is going to be alive for a long time to come. What I think the Hispanic population is saying is we need to learn English, and we will. But we also want to preserve the Spanish language because it has value. Plus, we have a cultural identity that when we see it reflected in the programming and the advertising, we feel more affinity to it."

The one common denominator among Hispanic groups is that these folks came to the United States with high hopes, dreams, and aspirations. They arrived with the work ethic of Kentucky coal miners, willing to take any job, any two jobs if necessary.

They were willing to risk their lives by wading across rivers, and taking high-risk jobs for a month's worth of paychecks, the amount of which would far surpass a year's earnings at home. They wanted what every American immigrant wants: A better life for themselves and their families, and they were willing to make huge sacrifices to get it.

The prospecting and marketeering that corporate America will have to do to reach the Hispanic market won't come without its pound of flesh, warned Korzenny, who has 25 years of experience in Hispanic marketing. "I think there are going to be a lot of casualties. It is a little bit like what happened with the high-tech boom. A lot of these Anglo agencies are daydreaming about the millions in (Hispanic) markets. They are going to waste their money. They don't understand the market."

"Anybody who has a sweet story can sell anything. So you are going to see a lot of junk, a lot of junk in the marketplace," he said. "Basically, what I see is a proliferation of people who are seeing the money opportunity and the gold rush. Companies are going to hire somebody who is promising expertise in the Spanish market. They're going to be sold on the idea that they can do Hispanics. But the majority of the clients do not have a good idea as to who can do a good job or not. It is a dangerous kind of situation. I think it is like any other consumer issue or customer issue. You have to shop around and be a good consumer."

The normal tenets of mass marketing won't always be effective in the Hispanic market, Korzenny said. What will, though, is to apply one of marketing's basic principles: Know your customer and understand the psyche of that customer.

"I've done thousands of studies over the years," Korzenny said. "...and I can testify with confidence that cynicism among Hispanics is much lower toward advertising (than that of the general public). There are good reasons for it. The Hispanic consumer is just beginning to be affluent, just beginning to be a true consumer in the American sense."

Korzenny is bullish on a Hispanic market that, in his estimation, is just starting to hit its stride. What's not to like, particularly when you consider the movement of Latinos into the middle- and upper-middle classes over the last 20 years? If the next 20 years bear any resemblance to the growth patterns of the previous two decades, today's economic numbers will pale in comparison.

Reasonable Levels of Corporate Investment

Research has indicated that "the value of the Hispanic market is still largely unrecognized" in American boardrooms. According to a 2004 study by the Association of Hispanic Advertising Agencies (AHAA), American companies had "only taken baby steps at shifting (advertising and marketing) allocations" toward the Hispanic market.

The objective of the study was to help corporations better allocate marketing and advertising resources to achieve maximum return. The study, which was conducted by the Santiago Solutions Group (SSG) using data provided by TNS Media Intelligence/CMR, looked at the spending trends of 671 of America's top national advertisers.

The study concluded that while some progress has been made, "American companies continue to show insufficient investments to spark sustained profitable revenue growth that is proportionate to the existing Hispanic purchasing power..."

In 2003 the AHAA calculated that American companies spent approximately $3.4 billion on Hispanic advertising, a 13 percent increase over 2002, and more than 240 percent over the $1.4 billion spent in 1997.

The top 10 companies on the AHAA list accounted for almost 25 percent ($787 million) of the total, with Procter & Gamble ($169 million) and Sears, Roebuck & Co. ($119 million) leading the way, followed in descending order by General Motors Corp. ($93 million), PepsiCo ($85 million), McDonald's Corp. ($64 million), Ford Motor Co. ($56 million), Toyota Motor Corp. ($56 million), Johnson & Johnson ($49 million), AT&T Corp. ($46 million), and Time Warner ($45 million).

Altogether, the top 50 companies on AHAA's list accounted for about 50 percent of the $3.4 billion spent in 2003. Twenty-five of those companies spent $1.1 billion (about a third of total expenditures) in Spanish-language television. Advertising allocations to Hispanic television media increased from 4.7 percent in 2002 to 7.4 percent in 2003. Allocations to Hispanic print media doubled, but the result only amounted to a mere 1 percent of total

---

Community Advocacy
Antonia Hernandez

Antonia Hernandez is nationally recognized for her commitment to the betterment of underserved communities, and for her expertise in civil rights and immigration issues. For 18 years she served as president and general counsel of the Mexican American Legal Defense and Education Fund (MALDEF). In February 2004, she became president and chief executive officer of the California Community Foundation. Hernandez began her career at the University of California, Los Angeles, as an attorney for the Los Angeles Center for Law and Justice, and the U.S. Senate Juris Doctor Committee counsel. She currently holds a trustee position at the Rockefeller Foundation, as well as board memberships for the Automobile Club of Southern California and Golden West Financial Corporation.

advertising expenditures (about $34 million).

The actual 2003 investment in Hispanic TV and print media, at 5.2 percent, was only about half of the AHAA-recommended 9 percent, a recommendation based on the percentage of U.S. markets that are Spanish speaking or bilingual. Also, it was only about one third of the 15 to 17 percent AHAA recommended for 19 designated market areas that have heavy Hispanic viewer and Spanish-language concentration.

According to AHAA, the Santiago Solutions Group studied the investment trends of major national advertisers relative to their competition and in correlation with the size, growth, and dollar value of the U.S. Hispanic consumer market. Arranging companies by category sectors, the AHAA created a report card determining which groups came closest to its recommended 9 percent goal. Of the 51 categories, only 10 either came close to the goal or exceeded it. Four categories (non-government organizations, fitness clubs, spas and diet programs, consumer electronic stores and audio/video manufacturers) allocated more than 15 percent of their promotional budgets for the Hispanic markets. The other six (food and drug stores, government, non-alcoholic beverages, household products, alcoholic beverages, and telecom services) spent between 8.8 percent and 11.1 percent of their budgets on Latino marketing.

Seven categories allocated 5 percent to 8 percent, which included restaurants, clothing and department stores, domestic car and truck dealers, furnishings and appliance stores, domestic car manufacturers, health aids, and gasoline and convenience stops. Fifteen categories fell into the 2 percent to 5 percent range, most notably appliance manufacturers, beauty aids, over-the-counter medicines, packaged foods, insurance, and credit cards.

The list of laggards bringing up the rear numbered 19, split between those that spent between 1 and 2 percent and those that fell below 1 percent. The former included seven sectors, most notably the Internet, business technology, banking and investment services, and educational institutions. The latter had 12 sectors, including pharmaceuticals, games, toys and hobby craft, telecommunications equipment, office equipment and supplies, and computer products. It is interesting to note that the computer products category didn't spend a dime.

Perhaps the most important revelation of the AHAA study was this: "As is true on a national level, if a marketer is currently under-allocating to reach Hispanics in a particular market, it means that the company is severely over-allocating (in other markets), resulting in a lower return on investment among non-Hispanic households."

Further, AHAA officials noted that over the next five years the continued shift in Latino demographics will create even more pressure to fix past allocation shortfalls. Manny Machado, president of AHAA, which represents about 70 Hispanic marketing agencies nationwide, said his organization released four studies in the past three years, and that there are "positive signs that AHAA's message is getting out there."

More than 20 companies in 2003 invested the highest percentage of ad budgets in Hispanic media, based on AHAA "right spend" recommendations, Machado said. They included PepsiCo, Sears Roebuck, U.S. government, Wal-Mart, Payless Shoesource, McDonald's, SABMiller, Texas Pacific Group, AT&T, State Farm Mutual, Colgate-Palmolive, Radio Shack, FoodMaker, Inc., Southwest Airlines, Domino's Pizza, Heineken, Bally Total Fitness, American Legacy Foundation, AARP, AMR, Avon, and Interbrew.

However, Machado said, "This is a small faction of all the corporations in the U.S. More companies need to realize the serious bottom-line advantages to targeting the Hispanic market, and then partner with the right agencies who can best sell their goods and services. It's as simple as that."

According to the AHAA study, Hispanic consumer demographics and purchasing behavior for categories such as children's over-the-counter remedies, baby products, personal electronics and personal care, and beauty and cosmetics, strongly suggested that American companies allocate from 10 percent to 25 percent of their total national business and marketing resources to the Hispanic Spanish/Bilingual market.

Companies in the businesses of fast food, apparel, home cleaning, grocery items, beer, non-alcoholic beverages, autos, home electronics, telecom, entertainment, travel, health information, and armed services should spend 7 to 13 percent. Those in financial investments, computers, and insurance, should step up to a level of about 7 percent.

In addition to looking at total national allocation levels, the AHAA recommended corporate America apportion even greater investments based on population density and language preferences in key Latino markets, like New York, Los Angeles, Miami, Chicago, Phoenix, and Houston. For example, while beer manufacturers and wireless providers should be allocating 10 percent of their overall national marketing resources to Spanish/bilingual Hispanics, they also should allocate about one-third of their Southern California resources and nearly half of their South Florida resources to reach local markets, the AHAA said.

Whether corporate America will adhere to the standards outlined by the AHAA is a story that will be written over the next few years. Some might argue that the return-on-investment is already attractive given that only $3.4 billion is being spent to coax billions from Hispanic wallets. But that presumes the current penetration of America's products and brands are already at lofty levels. And they probably are not – witness the lagging numbers in such key consumer categories as banking services, homeownership, computer ownership, Internet access services, and pharmaceutical needs.

It would also presume – albeit wrongly – that Hispanic population growth is slowing. This is certainly not the case, especially when one factors in the population growth rate of both American-born Hispanic youth and future waves of new immigrants.

It has been estimated that 400,000 illegal immigrants come to the U.S. each year, the vast majority from impoverished Mexico. And unless, by some miracle, Mexico comes up with national programs that provide jobs for its people, this immigrant inflow will not abate anytime soon. Mexico's current population stands at about 105 million. Projections indicate that by 2020 the Mexican population will climb to 128 million, and by 2030 to 142 million.

On the upside, there is evidence of an emerging middle class. A *Hispanic Business* study entitled "U.S. Hispanic Consumers in Transition: A Descriptive

Guide," released in 2003, showed that, in relative terms, Latino wealth was on the rise. The magazine's research arm, HispanTelligence, reported:

The mean income of Hispanic households grew from $32,359 in 1972 to $44,383 in 2001, a 37.2 percent increase.

Latino households in the lower income brackets ($34,900 or less) fell from 64.3 percent in 1972 to 51.8 percent in 2001.

Checking accounts grew 32 percent in value, while stocks and mutual fund shares grew 28.1 percent.

The proportion of Hispanic households earning more than $100,000 per year grew from 1.5 percent to 7 percent during the same period, meaning there are now more than 700,000 Latino households nationwide above that mark.

The number of middle-income Hispanic households ($35,000-$99,999) grew from 34.2 percent to 41.3 percent in 2001, a 20.8 percent increase, pushing the total of Latino households in this range to more than 4.13 million nationwide.

As the latter two groups evolve economically, and as others move into the middle- and upper-middle categories, the segment's overall aggregate wealth and disposable income naturally will grow. When combined with the number of New Latino immigrants arriving from Central and South America – who are more educated and have higher income-earning potential – the idea of Hispanic critical mass and purchasing power takes on an entirely new meaning.

Juan Solana, the chief economist of *Hispanic Business'* HispanTelligence, debunked the age-old argument that immigrants come to America primarily to avail themselves of public assistance and other welfare services. Hispanic incomes have been growing at an increasing rate, overall employment among Latinos has been on the rise since 2000, and more Hispanic women are working part-time and full-time jobs than ever before, all of which leads to a changing labor profile and increased household income.

"You cannot make that argument about public assistance and welfare," Solana said. "Statistically, the evidence is totally the opposite."

A report authored by John R. Logan of the Lewis Mumford Center for Comparative Urban and Regional Research at the University at Albany (N.Y.) showed that as of 2000, only 3 percent of all U.S. Hispanic immigrants were on public assistance. Among Mexicans, which constitute more than two-thirds of all Latino immigrants coming into the United States, the percentage was only 2.6 percent. It was even lower for the next two largest groups from Central and South America at 2.4 percent and 0.8 percent, respectively.

Global Insight, Inc., an economic and financial information service company, echoed Solana's explanation regarding employment among Hispanics. According to a 2003 report prepared for and sponsored by the Spanish-language television network Telemundo Communications Group., Hispanic employment rates continued to grow during the current downturn. Global Insight also reported that while economy-wide employment declined by 980,000 since 2000, Latino employment increased by 450,000.

Latino-Owned Businesses

Hispanic affluence has been further spurred by the number of Latino-owned businesses that started during 2000 and 2004. The number of Hispanic-owned firms is expected to exceed 2 million this year, a 33-percent jump since 2000.

Three out of four businesses will be concentrated in just four states – California, Texas, Florida, and New York – according to an Internal Revenue Service report. The top 10 metropolitan areas with the largest number of Latino-owned businesses are in one of those four states. Retail, service, skilled professional services, construction, and manufacturing make up 70 percent of Hispanic-owned business nationwide, according to the Latino Business Association, the country's largest Latino business organization with an active membership of more than 1,300.

Latino-owned firms are projected to generate revenues totaling $273 billion in 2004, according to Solana. He also projected that the number of firms will grow 7.6 percent annually, jumping to 3.2 million with revenues of more than $465 billion by 2010. "The strong growth indicates the increasingly vital role of Hispanic-owned firms in U.S. economic development," said Solana, adding that the service and financial sectors are expected to show the greatest growth.

With 2 million Latino-owned businesses today, and 3.2 million projected in six years – the income potential is staggering. These businesses will require office furniture, computers, software, copiers, fax machines, office telephones, mobile phones, accounting systems, banking services to handle payroll and operational expenses, company vehicles, consulting services, insurance plans, security systems – many of the products produced by companies at the bottom of AHAA's advertising list.

Hispanic Business' list of the 500 largest Hispanic-owned businesses of 2004 included 20 companies that generated revenues of more than $200 million in 2003. The top three on the list – Burt Automotive Network (automotive sales), in Centennial, Colorado, and Brightstar Corp. (telecommunications) and The Related Group of Florida (real estate) both of Miami – generated more than $1 billion in revenues each in 2003, with Burt Automotive topping the list at $1.63 billion. MasTech, Inc., a Pennsylvania-based consulting firm, fell out of the billion-dollar club in 2003 after its revenues dipped to $874 million, placing it fourth on the list.

As Joel Russell, senior editor at *Hispanic Business* told *USA Today* in May 2004, "Hispanic businesses are outgrowing the stereotype of the small mom-and-pop (store)."

In the same article, *USA Today* reported that a number of prominent companies moved into this largely small-business segment. For example, eBay announced the debut of the Entrepreneur's Center, a website partly in Spanish that helps aspiring small-business owners. Ford Motor also launched a similar site, as did technology giants IBM and Hewlett-Packard. The publication noted that, aside from being customers, these Hispanic business owners were "trendsetters" who, as tangential community role models, influenced the buying habits of the broader Latino market, particularly those who aspired to own a business, and those who were in the midst of kick-starting one.

Solana also noted that Hispanic women were the fastest growing influence in the Latino business community. Latinas wielded more power than Hispanic men, he said, proportionally in both professional and managerial positions (21.4 and 14 percent of the work force, respectively), and educational achievement (60 percent of bachelor's degrees awarded in 2000 were earned by Latinas). In comparison to their non-Hispanic female counterparts, Hispanic women were an average of 9.8 years younger. Yet they also lagged in job levels and pay, with a nearly $5,000 lower median annual income, Solana said.

By 2050, Solana said, the number of Hispanic women in the United States will reach almost 50 million, a growth spurt roughly two times the current Latina population. During the same time period, the total U.S. female population will grow only 62 percent, to about 207 million.

"What do these key findings mean for the future of Hispanic women? Hispanic women will have an increasing impact on the face of the U.S. economy that cannot be ignored — especially entrepreneurial and small-business ventures," Solana said. From 1997 to 2002, the number of Latina-owned businesses surged 39 percent. In 2002, Hispanic women were estimated to own 470,344 firms, employing 198,000 people and generating $24.9 billion in sales.

According to the Center for Women's Business Research, between 1997 and 2002 the number of privately held, majority-owned, minority-women-owned firms grew by 31.5 percent, outpacing the 14.3 percent growth rate among all women-owned firms, the 29.7 percent rate among all minority-owned firms, and the 6.8 percent growth of all U.S. firms.

The Hispanic Youth Market

Hispanic youth represent yet another opportunity for companies trying to gain a foothold into the Latino market. These young people are a powerful influence in the Hispanic household, often able to navigate fluidly between the Latino and American cultures, and between Spanish- and English-speaking worlds. Whether they came to the U.S. as immigrant children or are the offspring of first-generation immigrant parents, Latino youth help set the pace for assimilation and acculturation into American society.

While Hispanic youth may be greatly influenced by their friends and by American culture, there remains a strong push-pull effect that stems from an affinity for Hispanic core values and culture, both of which revolve around the family structure. They take pride in being diverse individuals, and they realize that they represent the best of both worlds.

According to the 2000 census, there were 12.3 million Hispanics under the age of 17, the largest of any ethnic youth group in the U.S. By 2005, they will overtake African American teens as the nation's largest ethnic population. They will account for about one in five of the under-18 age group, and 45 percent of all minority minors in the U.S., according to *Hispanic Business*. Recent research has found that:

Between 1993 and 2001, the Hispanic teen population grew 30 percent; the non-Hispanic teen population grew 8 percent during the same period. By 2020, the Hispanic teen population is expected to grow 62 percent compared to 10 percent growth in the number of teens overall (Nielsen Media Research).

Nearly 90 percent of all Hispanic teens lived in a household with families, compared to about 70 percent for the rest of the U.S. Almost half of all Latino teens listed watching television with their families as a favorite activity (*Hispanic Business*).

The average Latino teen spent about $320 a month, 4 percent more than the average non-Hispanic teen. Shopping malls (84 percent), supermarkets (80 percent), and discount chains (78 percent) were their most popular retail destinations (AHAA studies). This means that Hispanic teens hold $19 billion in spending power, most of which goes to clothing and jewelry. Other areas included music and entertainment, food and snacks, savings, gas and automobile expenses, and gaming and hobbies. The top five types of purchases made by Latino teens (related by sales volume) were entertainment, clothing, fast food, computer software, and toys (*Hispanic Business*).

Hispanic girls spent 60 percent more on makeup, 50 percent more on acne products, and twice as much on hair products as female teens in general (American Baby Group).

Hispanics tend to make shopping a family affair. More than a third (36 percent) said they preferred shopping with their families, and 30 percent said they liked shopping with their children, as compared to 29 percent and 26 percent, respectively, of the total population (*American Demographics*).

A quarter of Hispanics said their kids had a significant impact on the brands they bought. Hispanics were almost twice as likely as white consumers to go out of their way to find new stores (13 percent versus 7 percent), and would rather shop at national chains than local mom-and-pop stores (*American Demographics*).

Latino teens were tech savvy. Nearly 98 percent had Internet access, and spent more than five hours a day online (HispanTelligence). More than four in 10 Hispanic parents reported that their children asked them to purchase something they saw online (America Online/RoperASW survey).

Two-thirds of Hispanic parents surveyed believed it was important for their children to know how to use the Internet (America Online/RoperASW survey). Hispanic parents also believed being online had a positive effect on their children. Two-thirds said using the Internet strengthened their children's skills for entering the job market, and 77 percent said it had a positive effect on the quality of their child's homework (America Online/RoperASW survey).

PROMO magazine, in a 2004 article on marketing to Hispanic youth, noted that after years of neglect, marketers have begun to target this growing sector by integrating Latino characters into children's media, and licensing them to toy and apparel manufacturers. The magazine, which focuses on marketing trends and strategies, reported that Sesame Workshop – the creative force behind Sesame Street – was consistently at the forefront of bilingual programming. "With Sesame Street, we have always incorporated Spanish into the programming, as well as developing Hispanic characters," said Margaret Pepe, Sesame Street's director of licensing.

For example, *Plaza Sesamo*, the Spanish-language adaptation, airs weekly on PBS and TeleFutura, reaching 84 percent of U.S. Hispanic households. *PROMO* reported that *Plaza Sesamo*-inspired children's apparel was introduced for sale at 59 Mervyn's locations in February 2004. The children's line was scheduled to roll out at additional Mervyn's stores, as well as Wal-Mart, Kohl's, JCPenney, and Sears stores. "For us, the *Plaza Sesamo* brand is a way to tap into Hispanic consumers," Heather Hanssen, marketing director at Sesame Workshop told *PROMO*. "We plan to put a big push into this product."

PROMO also reported that Scholastic Entertainment planned to produce *The Misadventures of Maya and Miguel,* an animated comedy featuring 10-year-old Latino twins. The program will target 6- to 8-year-olds, and broadcast on PBS Kids in both English and Spanish five times a week.

Maya and Miguel will be backed by Scholastic's distribution in schools, reaching 53 million kids and 3.3 million teachers. Soft goods, including apparel, accessories, and bedding, will launch in spring 2005, with toys and hard goods projected to roll out in the fall of 2005.

"This is a call-to-action — there is clearly a need to enter the Hispanic market," Cheryl Gotthelf, executive project director for Scholastic Entertainment's *Clifford The Big Red Dog series,* told *PROMO*. "We developed original content with two goals: to celebrate cultural diversity and support Spanish language learning."

Nick Jr.'s *Dora the Explorer,* featuring a bilingual heroine, is the highest-rated pre-school show on commercial television among kids aged 2 to 5. Sara Levin, of Nickelodeon media relations, told *PROMO* that Nick Jr. has a history of introducing kids to different cultures. Similar shows, which will introduce more Hispanic characters, are in development. The Nick Jr. show teaches that speaking Spanish is both a valuable tool and a source of pride, Levin added.

Fisher-Price, the master toy licensee for *Dora the Explorer,* introduced new toys at Toy Fair in February, and planned to roll out Dora's Talking House, which incorporates bilingual phrases in an adobe-style play space.

Direct Marketing to Hispanics

As with any target market or special product, there is no overarching formula that guarantees success. In the Hispanic market, experts believe a multicultural approach has the greatest potential. The question is, how do you wrap your arms around an oak tree? The "low hanging fruit," as marketers like to call it, is within easy reach. But beyond that, what? How does a company's brand keep its competitive edge? Not everybody can be Proctor & Gamble, which in 2000 set up a 65-person bilingual team to target Hispanics. Or a Merrill Lynch, which can throw a 400-person unit together to figure out a way to expand its Hispanic investment accounts.

There is certainly no lack of information. Every month brings yet another report that slices and dices the Hispanic market. The challenge is to keep pace with the data. For example, when research for this book began, the most quotable annual purchasing figure for Hispanics was just below $600 billion. Within six months that number was revised several times, with the latest projection for 2004 now at $700 billion.

The data on the Hispanic market are overwhelming. Some of it is garden variety statistical information. Other reports are beginning to cast light on some of the challenges and pitfalls of marketing to Hispanic consumers. For example, at a time when direct mail efforts have waned among American consumers due to overkill, there are indications that Hispanics might respond more favorably to direct marketing than non-Hispanics. According to data from the Simmons Market Research Bureau, the average consumer receives 350 pieces of English-language direct mail per year, but Hispanic consumers receive only a tenth of that number. What's more, in 2002, 18 percent of Hispanics made a purchase based on a direct mail offer.

It's hard to believe that these findings pertain to Hispanics in general. Those who have been here for two or more generations are surely exposed to the daily onslaught of direct mail as much as other American consumers. But if the data focuses either on the waves of new Latino immigrants – many of whom are without an established address – or those who are trying to acculturate as quickly as possible, the opportunities for direct mail could indeed be wide open. The theory behind such a strategy is that new Spanish-dominant immigrants are likely to be more receptive, if not more susceptible, to direct marketing efforts than their English-dominant, Latino brethren, who have been hardened by overexposure.

Television advertising also fared better. Nielsen Media Research and Simmons, in separate studies, concluded that Hispanic viewers – particularly Spanish-dominant viewers – were more trusting, more receptive, and more likely to have purchasing decisions influenced by television ads than either English-dominant Hispanics or non-Hispanics. The Nielsen study, which was commissioned by Univision, the Spanish-language media company, also found:

According to previous research, seven in 10 Hispanic teens are bilingual or English-dominant, which means Hispanic teens in the 13- to 16-year-old category can be reached through English-language media. According to the Nielsen study, however, 52 percent of Hispanic viewers got purchase information directly from Spanish-language television, compared to 17

Politics
Octaviano Larrazolo, 1859-1930 and Dennis Chavez, 1888-1962
As the first Hispanic to serve in the U.S. Senate (17th congressional session 1928-29), Octaviano Larrazolo was instrumental in writing the New Mexico State Constitution. His service in the U.S. Senate laid the path for future Latino legislators to follow, such as Dennis Chavez of New Mexico, who served until his death in 1962. During his 27 years in office, Chavez championed civil rights reform, such as the Fair Employment Practices Commission Bill, which sought to terminate workplace discrimination based on race.

---

percent of Hispanic viewers of English-language TV. Only 7 percent of non-Hispanics got this information from English-language TV.

Thirty-six percent of Hispanics who watched Spanish-language television saw the entire commercial, as compared to 17 percent of Hispanics who watched English-language TV. Only 10 percent of non-Hispanics who watched English-language TV saw a commercial in its entirety.

Forty percent of Hispanics watching Spanish-language television discussed commercials with others, compared with only 7 percent of non-Hispanics watching English-language television. The Simmons study, which was based on English- and Spanish-language interviews of 25,398 Americans (including 8,221 Latinos), found Hispanic Spanish TV viewers had more faith in the advertising message, and were less likely than non-Hispanic English viewers to say TV advertising was "devious" or misleading. Spanish TV viewers were even more likely to find television advertising interesting and a frequent topic of discussion.

Hispanic Spanish-language TV viewers had a more positive view of advertising, and were more likely to feel it offered value. They were also less likely to find commercials annoying.

Finally, the Simmons study determined that Hispanic Spanish TV viewers were more likely to have purchasing decisions influenced by product advertising. For example, Hispanic Spanish TV viewers were 17 percent and 19 percent more likely to remember advertised products while shopping than non-Hispanic English TV viewers and the Hispanic English-only viewer, respectively. The same was true of decisions related to the purchase of products for their children (45 percent and 15 percent).

"Although the marketing community has come far in understanding the Hispanic market, it has yet to explore many areas of behavior, attitude and lifestyle," said Guadalupe Sierra, brand manager for Simmons' Hispanic Products. "These new National Consumer Study findings reflect how the right research tools can help companies identify some of the untapped and unique marketing opportunities among Hispanic consumers."

The Hispanic Online Potential

As of January 2004, there were almost 200 million Internet users in the United States. Of that total, 14 million were Hispanics, or 7 percent of all U.S. Internet users. With a total of 40 million Hispanics nationwide – plus another 6 to 8 million undocumented immigrants – that number represents a market which is almost completely untapped. But as the Hispanic middle class continues to emerge and more households purchase computers, those numbers are changing, as is the profile of the Hispanic user.

In 2000, only 47 percent of all Hispanic households owned a computer. That number has risen in the past four years to 56 percent. While 56 percent is still low when compared to the rest of America, one has to remember that access to the Internet is not limited to computers in Latino homes. Many Latino youths access the Internet via computers at schools, libraries, or friends' homes.

According to Cheskin Research, wired Hispanics in 2000 differed significantly from those who were not online. They were better educated (14.4 years of school versus 9.5), younger (34 versus 40), and much more likely to own a credit card (75 percent versus 39 percent). Latino Web surfers also consumed fewer hours of Spanish-language media a week than non-users (13 versus 24).

Here again, language played an important role. "While English content can and does reach large numbers of Hispanics, to fully reach U.S. online Hispanics, marketers must also provide relevant Spanish language content." said Richard Israel, former vice president of comScore Hispanic Solutions.

The country's major consumer banking and lending institutions were among the earliest investors in Spanish-language content and online Hispanic marketing. Banks had a 25 percent increase in U.S. Hispanic visitors during 2002, compared to an increase of 10 percent among general Internet users. In fact, four sites more than doubled the number of visitors. Each of them featured Spanish-language content.

Not only did the number of visitors to Hispanic bank sites increase, so did their engagement level. Bank of America drew 51 percent more Hispanic visitors than in 2002, and recorded a remarkable 68 percent increase in page views. Hispanic use of Citigroup's site rose 49 percent, compared with 22 percent for non-Hispanics. Capital One and WellsFargo.com both recorded increases of 29 percent or more.

The second annual American Online/RoperASW U.S. Hispanic

Cyberstudy, which was released this year, confirmed those findings. It found that language remained a significant barrier among Hispanics who used the Internet away from home. More than half cited the lack of Spanish content as a reason for not going online. Forty-nine percent said there weren't enough Spanish sites and activities online to interest them. Almost half of Hispanic online consumers who spoke at least some Spanish said they wanted more advertising in Spanish. Thirty-three percent said they paid more attention to advertisements in Spanish; 23 percent said advertising in Spanish made them more likely to buy a given product. Fifteen percent said they almost bought something online, but changed their minds due to language difficulty.

Hispanics used the Internet far more frequently than the general online population to listen to music (54 percent versus 30 percent), buy a car (6 percent versus 2 percent), or communicate via instant messaging (64 percent versus 48 percent). Hispanic online users also adopted advanced wireless features. For example, 30 percent of online cell phone users used them for instant messaging, compared with just 9 percent of the general online population.

Latino parents saw the Internet as a powerful tool for improving the education and career prospects of their children. Seventy percent said the Internet improved the ability of their children to get into college; 79 percent said it had a positive effect on the skills their children will need for a successful career.

"These trends indicate that the Internet is playing an increasingly important role in Hispanics' lives," Israel said. "Many are developing online preferences and loyalties that will last well into the future."

Other findings from the AOL/Roper study included:

Twenty percent of Hispanics have been online at home less than six months, compared with just 6 percent of the general at-home online population. Forty-two percent had an Internet connection at home for less than two years, compared to 15 percent of the general online population.

More than half of offline Hispanics expected to get an Internet connection at home within the next two years. Seventeen percent expected to do so within the next six months.

More than a third of online Hispanics regularly or occasionally downloaded music files (39 percent) compared with 27 percent of the general online population. Thirty-four percent regularly or occasionally watched video clips, compared with 23 percent of the general online population.

Almost half (43 percent) said they go online and watch TV at the same time. More than a third actually viewed the Internet as an alternative to TV, reporting that they watched TV less since they started going online.

Hispanics who shopped online spent an average of $480 in the past three months, compared to $577 for the general online population. Forty-three percent said they regularly or occasionally shopped online; 52 percent said the ability to shop online was a reason they got an Internet connection at home.

More than half (59 percent) viewed the Internet as the best source to compare prices (versus 50 percent in 2002), and half (51 percent) said it was the best place to get information for making a final brand decision (versus 40 percent in 2002).

Those who purchased a car in the past three years were far more likely than the general online population to use the Internet to choose features and options for a new car (46 percent versus 30 percent); find the location of a car dealer (45 percent versus 25 percent); and make an actual new car purchase (12 percent versus 3 percent).

More than half (54 percent) used the Internet to research health care products, while 19 percent shopped for or bought pharmaceuticals – a number almost twice that of the general online population (11 percent).

Fifty-two percent used the Internet to make travel arrangements (52 percent versus 40 percent).

Nearly 61 percent used the Internet in the past three years to do one or more of the following: pay a bill, do online banking, compare insurance rates, or open a checking account.

Almost half send money to family members living outside the U.S., but only 5 percent used the Internet for the transaction.

Twenty-six percent of online Hispanics said they used coupons received via the Internet.

Sears, Roebuck & Co., which spent $119 million in Spanish-language advertising in 2003, recently reported it was dismantling its stand-alone multicultural marketing department and merging the unit into its general marketing operations. According to *Advertising Age*, the move "has sparked industry debate about whether multicultural advertising efforts should be conducted from separate silos or whether they are more effectively managed as part of the overall marketing organization."

Was the Sears decision a good move? Will other companies follow Sears' lead, or will they continue their segmented approaches to the Hispanic marketplace. Sears was a longtime player in the Hispanic market, often taking the lead as a multicultural marketer. Is this recent decision a short-term strategy to help Sears buy time and weather a potentially slow sales period, or is it a longer-term tactic that could influence other retailers? Perhaps company executives figured out a way to dovetail the multicultural piece of the operation into its overall marketing engine where it is efficient. Only time will tell, as will the company's bottom line results. In the meantime, it could also mean an opportunity for another company waiting to step in. Korzenny said there will be companies that will lose their way. But there also will be other companies that will find their niche and capitalize accordingly.

CHAPTER SIX

An American Dream Without a Home

The Hispanic community is one of the most dynamic in the country. Its members are the youngest ethnic minority; fully half of Latino heads of household are under 40. Their population rates are up and their economic power is growing. As the fastest growing ethnic group in the country and with an emerging middle class, the Hispanic community is on deck to be a key driver of household growth over the next decade.

This should mean that more Latino families are becoming homeowners, that they are finding their piece of the American dream and setting roots deep into their communities. But it doesn't. Latino homeownership rates lag far behind those of other groups.

Homeownership remained the single most important source of accumulated wealth for minority and lower income households. It was the ultimate goal, the proof of success and permanency in American society. Yet only 47 percent of Hispanics owned their own homes in 2002 compared with 68 percent of all U.S. households. "For low and moderate income families, the difference between renting and owning a home marks a separation between getting by from day to day and building up the equity that may be later used as collateral for an investment in higher education or starting a business, to guarantee a secure retirement, and to pass on increased wealth and security to the next generation," reported *The Great Divide*, a study by the Association of Community Organizations for Reform Now (ACORN), a grassroots consumer advocacy group and loan counseling agency for the U.S. Department for Housing and Urban Development (HUD). "For communities, it is often the difference between absentee landlords and committed neighbors. Without access to credit on fair terms, communities have no hope of emerging into strong, stable, and safe neighborhoods."

This is not to say that Latinos haven't made important economic strides. There are healthy signs of growing affluence. The trouble is that the typical markers of success – homeownership, education rates, rise in income levels – are often obscured by the influx of new immigrants. This is especially true with homeownership; while the overall rate of homeownership looks flat, buried in the statistics is evidence of significant material gains made by the older members of the community.

This phenomenon also skews the view of rising income and education levels. The last 20 years have seen substantial progress by the native-born Latino. Unfortunately, these gains tend to be counterbalanced by increases in the number of poor, foreign-born Latino households.

In fact, *BusinessWeek* reported in March 2004 that Latinos represented the fastest growth in homeownership of any group in the U.S. In a cover story on Hispanics, the magazine wrote that 10 million new homes will be built by the end of the decade. Half of those homes are expected to be purchased by minorities, and more than half will be purchased by Hispanics. This will result in almost 3 million new Latino homeowners.

Those who want to become one of the 3 million will have some barriers to negotiate. For instance, potential Latino homebuyers, especially first generation, may not have a bank account or credit card, and therefore no credit history. They may be intimidated by the complex maze that is the homebuying process. Low-income levels could mean they can't save for a down payment or manage long-term debt. They may not have access to American financial institutions or understand the requirements to open a checking or savings account. Fannie Mae's 2003 National Housing Survey found that while most Americans view homeownership as a safe investment with upside potential, there are important gaps that must be addressed if minority homeownership is to catch up with the rest of the population.

Financing

One of the most serious concerns is a reluctance to enter into formal relationships with American financial institutions. This can be attributed, at least in part, to the "myth of impermanence," the belief that one comes to America just long enough to make a decent amount of money and return home. Why open a bank account when it's more expedient to conduct business in cash, paying bills at the grocery store, and cashing paychecks at fee-based check-cashing agencies. These potential homebuyers are "unbanked." They do not have bank accounts or credit cards, and therefore no way to establish a credit history.

There are those who believe they have to be naturalized citizens before they can open bank accounts or establish credit. They don't realize banks can now accept, at their discretion, either the Mexican *Matricula Consular* or an IRS tax identification card in lieu of a driver's license or social security card. According to a 2004 study funded by Freddie Mac and conducted by The Tomás Rivera Policy Institute (TRPI) at the University of Southern California, this kind of confusion existed in spite of the fact that the majority of the study's respondents had lived in the U.S. for more than a decade.

Finally, potential Hispanic homebuyers may not make enough money. They may struggle to save a down payment, or have a level of income that doesn't allow them to qualify for a loan. Others aren't sure they can manage the long-term debt that comes with homeownership. Low wages and financial remittance to one's country of origin also can reduce the potential homebuyer's income to the point that a bank account and the fees typically associated with it are an unnecessary extravagance.

Of those who did begin the homebuying process, more than half failed to complete it, saying it was more expensive than they initially thought. Fannie

Mae's 2003 National Housing Survey found that affordability concerns were primarily driven by a lack of savings. The report also cited credit concerns, such as the ability to get a low-cost mortgage without an adequate credit history. In fact, credit concerns were the second leading reason (39 percent) renters overall had for not buying a home, ranking just behind cost. Credit concerns were an even bigger issue for minority households; 49 percent of English-speaking Hispanics and 46 percent of Spanish-language Hispanics cited credit concerns as the primary reason they had not yet bought a home.

Information

Potential Latino buyers did not understand how U.S. financial institutions functioned, or how real estate and credit markets worked. The 2004 TRPI study, titled *El Sueño de su Casa: The Homeownership Potential of Mexican-Heritage Families,* showed a significant barrier to homeownership was the lack of information. For those who spoke little English, it was almost impossible to understand the complexity of the homebuying process without help from others. The result was that prospective homebuyers were often uninformed or misinformed about how to get started, how to find a house, make offers, negotiate, qualify for a mortgage, or secure financing, and had difficulty finding someone they trusted to advise them.

The good news, according to the study, was that survey respondents trusted the formal gatekeepers to provide accurate information. The most useful sources of information were real estate professionals, followed by friends, co-workers, family members, or relatives. These future homebuyers said they also got information from television, the Internet, and newspaper advertisements. Homebuying seminars or classes, and financial institutions, such as banks, were among the least utilized sources of information.

According to the Fannie Mae survey, only 18 percent of Spanish-language-dominant Hispanics claimed an above average understanding of the homebuying process, compared with a third of Americans overall. Sixty-five percent of English-dominant Hispanics and only 27 percent of Spanish-dominant Hispanics knew a mortgage did not require a 30-year commitment, as compared with 74 percent of all respondents. Sixty-four percent of English-speaking Hispanics and only 22 percent of Spanish-dominant Hispanics knew it was not necessary to have a perfect credit rating to qualify for a mortgage, compared with 73 percent of all respondents. Fifty-five percent of English-dominant Hispanics and only 39 percent of Spanish-dominant Hispanics knew it was not necessary to stay in the same job for at least five years to qualify for a mortgage, compared with 65 percent of all respondents.

"This year's survey will help us achieve our expanded American Dream Commitment to underserved families by helping us understand more about the minority homeownership gaps and the best strategies to close them," said Fannie Mae Chairman and Chief Executive Officer Franklin D. Raines. Fannie Mae's goal is to create 6 million new homeowners (including 1.8 million minority families) over the next 10 years, help families keep their

---

Business
James J. Padilla
James J. Padilla is the chairman of automotive operations and chief operating officer for Ford Motor Co., one of the top five corporations ranked by Fortune magazine. He has contributed to innovation in the global automotive business, and improved automotive marketing, manufacturing, and engineering in more than 200 countries worldwide. He was named a Fellow by the National Academy of Engineering, given the "Engineer of the Year" by the Hispanic Engineer National Achievement Awards Conference, and received the Ohtli medal for his dedication to the betterment of the Mexican people — the highest honor a Mexican descendent can receive from the Mexican government. Padilla played an instrumental role in North American operations for Ford, serving as division president and group vice president. He began his career as a White House Fellow in 1978, came to Ford in 1966 as a quality control engineer, and later became director of Engineering and Manufacturing Cars, Ltd.

homes, and expand the supply of affordable homes where they are needed most. Fannie Mae officials said they have earmarked $2 trillion over the next decade to boost homeownership among low- to moderate-income Americans.

Language

Language barriers were a significant roadblock for Hispanic consumers. The inability to communicate made the homebuying process particularly intimidating. The TRPI study, which focused exclusively on Latinos of Mexican origin since they account for 67 percent of all Latinos living in the U.S., found that three-quarters of both prospective homebuyers and recent homeowners preferred to communicate in their own language. Of those who were in the early stages of the homebuying process, 51 percent said they were not comfortable expressing themselves in English; 40 percent of those who had either purchased a home or were well into the process said they would rather communicate in Spanish.

These results were supported by the Urban Institute, which found that about 60 percent of legal immigrants who were currently eligible to naturalize were "limited English proficient." About 40 percent said they spoke English "not well" or "not at all." The solution here may be to translate informational documents and brochures into Spanish, and employ bilingual staff to better serve this community.

Discrimination

Concerns over discriminatory barriers were substantiated in two ACORN reports. In *The Great Divide*, ACORN revealed that while the homeownership rate in the U.S. rose to 68 percent in 2002– it has risen every year since 1993 –the national figure masked continued disparities between the experiences of white Americans and those of Hispanics and blacks. Hispanic families made more progress, ACORN said, but they started from farther behind, and still had the lowest rate of homeownership in the country. "A major factor contributing to the homeownership gap is that minority and lower income families experience continuing, and in many cases growing, inequalities in obtaining the financing necessary to purchase a home. In addition, the prevalence in minority communities of subprime refinance lending, with its inflated prices and attendant predatory abuses, puts an increasing number of homeowners at risk of losing their homes."

The report looked in detail at the denial rates and ratios for borrowers of different races and incomes when they applied for conventional and government-backed home loans, as well as at the number of originations and applications for such loans. "It is impossible to overstate the damage caused by the continuing inequalities in access to mortgage credit," the report said. "It is also important to note that more detailed analysis suggests that the continued disparity in access to mortgage loans cannot be explained away by the argument that minority applicants have less good credit."

In the most thorough study available, ACORN said researchers at the Federal Reserve Bank of Boston examined individual applications, controlling for credit, income, and other factors. The Federal Reserve Bank found that, even once differences in credit were taken out of the picture, black and Latino applicants were significantly more likely to be denied a mortgage loan than similarly situated white applicants.

Among other things, *The Great Divide* showed that minority applicants for conventional loans were rejected significantly more often than whites, and

---

Media
Ignacio Lozano, 1886-1953
Ignacio Lozano is regarded as a pioneer in Spanish-language publishing. In 1913, Lozano founded the Spanish-language newspaper La Prensa in San Antonio, Texas. Thirteen years later he founded La Opinión newspaper in Los Angeles, which remains the oldest and largest Spanish-language daily newspaper in the nation. Under the supervision of his grandchildren, Ignacio Lozano's media publication dynasty continues to provide the Hispanic communities with a trustworthy source of news, information, and current events.

that the disparity has grown over time, with rejection ratios in 2002 higher than in 2001, and higher than they were in 1997.

Latinos were turned down 1.63 times more often than whites in 2002, up from 1.53 times in 2001, and 1.49 times in 1997.

The Great Divide also showed that minorities of all incomes were rejected more often than whites, a disparity that increased as income level increased. Minorities with higher incomes were denied more often than whites with lower incomes. Upper-income and upper-middle income Latinos were twice as likely (2.13 and 2.07, respectively) to be turned down than were upper-income and upper-middle income whites.

Moderate-income Latinos were 1.63 times more likely to be turned down than moderate-income whites, while low-income Latinos were 1.26 times more likely to be turned down than low-income whites.

Predatory Lending

A second ACORN report titled, *Separate and Unequal: Predatory Lending in America,* was even more critical of the nation's lending institutions, alleging that the elderly, the communities of color, and low-income neighborhoods were the most likely targets of predatory lenders, which the report defined as "mortgage and finance companies that make loans with high interest rates, exorbitant fees, and other harmful terms, often through fraudulent and deceptive methods."

The ACORN study spotlighted the practices surrounding subprime lending. These were loans given to people who were unable to obtain a conventional loan at the standard bank rate due to credit problems or other circumstances. Subprime loans carried higher interest rates to compensate for the potentially greater risk these borrowers represented. This kind of risk-based pricing fulfilled an important market need, but at times spilled over into fraud. "While not all subprime lenders are predatory, just about all predatory loans are subprime, and the subprime industry is a fertile breeding ground for predatory practices. Predatory lending occurs when loan terms or conditions become abusive or when borrowers who should qualify for credit on better terms are targeted instead for higher cost loans," the report said.

The number of subprime loans has soared since the early 1990s. In 1993, just over 100,000 subprime refinance and home purchase loans were originated, compared to 1.36 million subprime loans in 2002. Some industry analysts project that the subprime loan volume will increase again through 2004.

The rise in subprime and predatory lending was most dramatic in minority communities. According to *Separate and Unequal*, subprime lending, with its higher prices and potential for abuse, was becoming the dominant form of lending in minority communities. According to ACORN, that shouldn't have been the case. "Fannie Mae has estimated that as many as half of all borrowers in subprime loans could have instead qualified for a lower cost mortgage. Freddie Mac suggested a somewhat lower, but still extremely large figure – that as many as 35 percent of borrowers who obtained mortgages in the subprime market could have qualified for a prime loan."

Too often the higher rate subprime loans were loaded with features like high fees, large and extended prepayment penalties, insurance policies, or expensive membership plans financed into their loans – which cost borrowers even more of their equity. Over the course of a 30-year mortgage, consumers needlessly paid thousands of dollars more for a loan that should have qualified for an "A" rating.

"When a borrower with good credit loses substantial equity when being refinanced into an excessive rate, they are frequently left without enough equity to refinance with another lender into a more reasonable rate," the report said. "Borrowers are also often trapped in loans when lenders or servicers damage their credit scores by falsely reporting late payments and inflated loan amounts; sometimes the simple fact of taking out a subprime loan or a home-equity line of credit – regardless of a borrower's repayment record – can damage a borrower's credit score."

"Those borrowers who are not in a position to qualify for an 'A' loan are also routinely overcharged in the subprime market, with rates and fees that reflect what a lender or broker thinks they can get away with, rather than any careful assessment of the actual credit risk," ACORN reported. "These loans too are often loaded with additional abusive features like financed credit insurance, hidden balloon payments, and mandatory arbitration clauses. Such borrowers often find themselves trapped in high rate loans even once they have improved their credit. Many borrowers are also repeatedly solicited and repeatedly refinanced into high rate loans, losing equity through every transaction."

Although some in the lending industry argued that the higher costs of subprime loans were reflective of borrowers with a high-risk profile and low credit ratings, the argument did not wash with Fannie Mae officials. "Fannie Mae has stated that the racial and economic disparities in subprime lending cannot be justified by credit quality alone. According to Fannie Mae, loans to lower-income customers perform at similar levels as loans to upper-income customers; indeed, research suggests that mortgages to low- and moderate-income borrowers perform better than other mortgages when the lower prepayment risk is taken into account."

Among its findings, the *Separate and Unequal* also discovered:

Subprime lenders continued to originate growing numbers of refinance loans. In 2002, subprime lenders originated 933,025 refinance loans, an increase of 33 percent over 2001. Prime lenders originated 8 million refinance loans in 2002, an increase of 24 percent from 2001.

Subprime lending increased at a faster rate than prime lending over the past 10 years, and its growth is accelerating. In conventional lending, subprime lenders originated 427,878 loans in 2002, a 44 percent increase from 2001. Prime lenders originated 3.7 million conventional loans in 2002 compared with 3 million in 2001, a smaller increase of 23 percent.

Almost 20 percent of the home loans received by Latinos in 2002 were from subprime lenders. In contrast, only 7.8 percent of the loans received by whites were from subprime lenders.

ACORN maintained that a lack of access to prime loans played a large role in the nearly 25 percent homeownership gap between white and minority households dating back four decades. That disparity remains virtually unchanged, with three-quarters of white households owning their own homes, compared to less than half of African-American and Latino families. Predatory lending threatens to reverse any progress that may have been made in increasing homeownership rates among minority and lower income families, according to the ACORN report. "Rather than strengthening neighborhoods by providing needed credit based on this accumulated wealth, predatory lenders have contributed to the further deterioration of neighborhoods by stripping homeowners of their equity and overcharging those who can least afford it, leading to foreclosures and vacant houses."

These practices, along with problems of language, and a lack of information, income, or a relationship with a financial institution, can all combine to create a situation in which Hispanic families have to rely on relatives or friends to act as proxy buyers. Barriers such as these also create a community of consumers who believe their only option is to deal with marginal institutions or individuals who charge high fees or interest rates, and do not report to credit repositories.

The Latino community is not a "self-editing" population – its members do not opt out of the housing market by choice. Most Hispanics expressed a strong desire to buy a home, but were unable to accomplish it for reasons that, with the exception of resolving residency status, seemed beyond their control. The result is an overall confidence gap between minorities and the general public over whether they can successfully complete the homebuying process. This gap is magnified by concerns over other factors, such as future home price increases.

According to the TRPI study, Hispanic homeownership rates could reach 53 percent by 2010, an increase of 2.2 million, if real estate professionals and community organizations addressed these barriers. Some efforts are already in place. For example, mortgage lenders are implementing programs that will enable them to better assess risk, and target their products to specific populations. The federal government has enacted measures that require mortgage accessibility and fair treatment of ethnic minorities and low-income households.

Barriers to homeownership cut across all generations and groups.

Solutions that begin the process of breaking them down will have a significant impact on the ability of other immigrant and minority groups to successfully negotiate the path to homeownership.

CHAPTER SEVEN

Media: Shaping the Images

Communication is the product of the century. It is global and instantaneous. Perceptions and opinions are formed in seconds, and too often are based on audio clips and sound bites, a few images, and maybe a few hundred words. The result is that the image of Latinos becomes the default mechanism of news programs that show Latinos crossing the border and challenging border patrols, or Latinos as part of a drug cartel.

The depiction of Hispanics by the media is crucial. With Latinos comprising the largest minority segment, and with that segment growing, it is incumbent on the American media to provide an accurate picture if society is to understand, accept, and appreciate Latinos as contributing members. For example, does the image of illegal Mexicans jumping over a wall at the U.S.-Mexico border summarize the story of Latinos in America? No, but it makes the evening news. During the Los Angeles riots in 1992, a local television anchor provided commentary as a video clip showed a group of what appeared to be Hispanics looting a grocery store. His thoughtful comment: "They certainly *looked* like Illegals."

Latinos have assimilated into every corner of American society. Yet their portrayal by the media is often skewed toward what the late Bob Maynard called "circus coverage." According to Maynard, an African American who pioneered discussions of diversity and the media, and who served on the editorial board at *The Washington Post*, and as editor of the *Oakland Tribune*, the only time the minority community is covered, at least by the national print media, is when it does something weird or criminal.

As recently as December 2003, a study by the National Association of Hispanic Journalists showed that television's evening newscasts covered Latinos mostly by focusing on crime and immigration stories. For the eighth straight year, the association's "National Brownout Study" found inadequate coverage of the nation's fastest growing minority. The report found 120 Latino-related stories in approximately 16,000 that aired on the major network newscasts in 2002 – less than 1 percent.

Hispanics are not fully represented on the other side of the fence either, i.e., as members of the media. Minority journalists struggle to rise from beat reporter to positions of power where they can help to steer coverage toward a more accurate portrayal of the Hispanic community. It is a function not of a glass ceiling, but a concrete one. This is true even in the face of the American Society of Newspaper Editors' Mission Statement on diversity: "To cover communities fully, to carry out their role in a democracy, and to succeed in the marketplace, the nation's newsrooms must reflect the racial diversity of American society in 2025 or sooner. At a minimum, all newspapers should employ journalists of color and a newspaper should reflect the diversity of its community."

The originally target date of this goal, which was adopted by the ASNE in 1978, was the year 2000. By 1996 minorities only accounted for 11.02 percent of the staff in newsrooms throughout the country, less than half of what the minority population count was at the time. In response, the ASNE adjusted its goal to the year 2025.

According to the ASNE 1999 Newsroom Employment Census, minorities comprised 11.55 percent of the reporters, copy editors, photographers, graphic artists, and supervisors at U.S. daily newspapers. On the other hand, minorities comprised an estimated 28.4 percent of the U.S. population. Diversity improved by nearly half of one percent in 2002, but the growth of minority journalists to 12.53 percent of newsroom staff lagged behind the 31.1 percentage of minorities in the U.S. population.

The good news in diversity, according to the ASNE 2002 annual census, was that the number of newspapers with no minorities dropped by nearly 100, from 471 to 373, meaning that 60 percent of the daily newspapers responding to the survey had minority staffers. The bad diversity news was that to reach parity, newspapers must increase their percentage of minorities in the newsroom by 229 percent if they are to mirror the projected U.S. minority population of 38 percent by 2025.

Diversity in the American media not only affects the coverage of Latinos, but also whether television, radio, and print serve the needs of the Hispanic community. The industry continues to grapple with the Hispanic market, seemingly unaware of how to serve it, or how to tap into the community's burgeoning buying power. The growth of the Spanish language media can be seen as a response to the mainstream media's inability to capture the Spanish-language market. Since the television rating system changed to better reflect cable viewing and non-mainstream channels, some remarkable numbers have shown up. For example, in a given week, several of the top-rated shows in markets like Los Angeles, New York, Miami or Chicago were Univision television shows. In addition, Univision's national newscasts typically had more viewers than the three English-language networks combined. Or consider *La Opinión*, the nation's largest Spanish-language daily newspaper. Located in Los Angeles, it has successfully covered the Latino community for 77 years.

Since 1990 the number of Latino-oriented publications has grown from 742 to 1,256, with 84 percent of those in Spanish. In 1999, it was called a "revolution in Hispanic print." Publications aimed at Latino consumers hit the newsstands in record numbers. They were targeted toward a market worth a reported $340 million in spending power, according to the National Association of Hispanic Publications. Even then, however, advertising in Latino media was less than 1 percent of almost $200 million spent on advertising overall in the previous year.

The Spanish-language media has continued to grow, and garner more of business's advertising dollars. In the first quarter of 2004, four Spanish-language daily newspapers started publication. General interest magazines, created by smart, young imaginative Latinos, are succeeding like never before.

Hispanics have not fared well in their representation in television or film. In early 2004 a non-profit organization called Children Now issued a report

---

Sports Entertainment
Arturo Moreno
In 2003, Arturo Moreno became the owner of the Angels Baseball Club of Anaheim, California, and the first Hispanic to own a major league franchise. In addition, he is a part owner of the Phoenix Suns, and is a former minority investor in the Arizona Diamondbacks. Noted as a "self-made millionaire," Moreno graduated from the University of Arizona and made an impression in the business industry while working for Outdoor Systems, a renowned billboard and outdoor advertising company. Forbes Magazine has estimated Moreno's net worth at more than $940 million.

---

titled *Fall Colors: Prime Time Diversity Report* that analyzed diversity in prime time television programming. The report examined prime time shows of the six major broadcast networks for the 2003-2004 season. It was conducted on the premise that 40 percent of American youth 19-years-old and under are children of color. The report concluded that these youths comprised the most racially diverse population in the country, yet their diversity was not reflected on prime time television. "When certain groups are privileged and others are excluded it sends a message especially to young viewers that these groups are valued differently by society," the report said.

The report analyzed five years of programming, and found that:

> The percentage of Latino characters rose from 4 percent of the total prime time population in 2001, to 6.5 percent in 2003.

> The percentage of Latino opening credits and characters increased threefold, from 2 percent in 2001, to 6 percent in 2003.

> Nearly 73 percent of all prime time characters were white.

> Although situation comedies were the most popular among youths,

they were the least diverse, most segregated shows on prime time.

Although there has been progress in increasing Latinos' presence in prime time, they were too often cast as characters with low-status occupations.

The report concluded that "the world of prime time entertainment on the six broadcast networks continued to fall short of reflecting the rich diversity of our society."

Hispanic participation in film also has been a long, slow climb. Sal Lopez, an actor in Los Angeles for 20 years, said that even in the cinematic capitol of the world, Latinos are not always accurately portrayed or appropriately cast. "Isn't it a shame that here we have one of the most powerful mediums in the world, and we still have such a long way to go in portraying Latinos correctly," Lopez said.

For Lopez and a growing number of Hispanic actors, the inability to be considered for roles has forced them to investigate other creative paths. Lopez, for example, produced and directed "Luminaries" in 2000. Adapted from the play, "Luminarias," the story evolved around a group of young, mid-level professional women sifting through the available male population for the "right" one. It was a theme that had been explored in mainstream film many times, only this time, the protagonists were Latinas.

Award-winning playwright and filmmaker Luis Valdez faced a host of problems when trying to develop and cast a movie based on Mexican artist Frida Kahlo's life. Valdez had already produced and directed a number of plays, including "Zoot Suit," a re-telling of the Sleepy Lagoon Murder in Los Angeles in the 40s. The play ran for two years in Los Angeles, and received critical acclaim when it opened in New York. Valdez later produced *La Bamba*, a movie about the life of singer Richie Valens.

In 1992 while trying to develop the film, *Frida and Diego*, Valdez became the target of protesting Latino actors and actresses when he announced he had cast Italian actress Laura San Giacomo in the lead role. A portion of Hispanic Hollywood reacted strongly, insisting that a Latina had to play the part. Valdez ultimately abandoned the project. It was almost a decade before Mexican-born Salma Hayek wrote and produced "Frida" in 2002.

In May 1999, The Tomás Rivera Polity Institute issued the results of a report commissioned by the Screen Actors Guild (SAG) titled, *Missing In Action, Latinos In and Out of Hollywood.*

"A vast market remains largely untapped by Hollywood: Latinos, who are active consumers of movies, television and video and represent a fast-growing audience with immense buying power," the report said. "The key to reaching that market is already in the industry's hands: the national pool of Latino talent in front of the camera."

According to SAG, whose membership at the time was made up of 4,852 Latinos, 9,566 African Americans, and 73,358 non-Hispanic whites, the study was designed to fill a void of information about Hispanics. It revealed some interesting characteristics:

Latino audiences for movies were split. U.S.-born Latinos were avid moviegoers, while foreign-born Latinos were less likely to see films in theaters.

Latinos were more likely to see films starring Latino actors than they were to see films that were equally popular but did not star Latinos. (This was recently contradicted by a later TRPI study, whose respondents were made up largely of first-generation Latinos, and who said that a Latino in a television show was not enough reason to watch it.)

The reports recommended:
- Promotion of color-blind casting
- Educating behind-the-camera decision-makers
- Increasing Hispanic programming
- Playing a more aggressive role in promoting Latino inclusiveness in the entertainment industry

In May of 2000 SAG and TRPI issued another report, this time titled, *Still Missing: Latinos In and Out of Hollywood.* The report was presumably a continuation and conclusion of the previous effort. "A year later, new research bolsters those findings (of 1999) and adds new ones," the report said.

Latinos emerged as one of the most underrepresented groups in television, movies, and other entertainment. Latino SAG members reported working only one day per month in the previous year. Thirty percent reported no work at all. Many believed the lack of work was the result of stereotyping by casting directors and other decision-makers.

"When one considers the history of the depiction of ethnic and racial groups within motion pictures, one sees almost a century of abuse in this regard," wrote film historian Allen L. Woll in 1988. "From the dawn of films virtually all ethnic groups have been stereotyped on the screen. Yet it is impossible to blame motion pictures alone for the perpetuation of these derogatory images. Most existed previously in literature and the graphic arts."

In a 1988 issue of *Media&Values*, a quarterly publication from the Center for Media Literacy, Woll wrote that "as the first mass media in the United States, movies spread distorted and often negative images of blacks, Mexican Americans, Irish, Chinese and Italians and others throughout the world."

Ironically, Woll cited World War II as a period when major advances were made in eliminating derogatory ethnic portrayals — a deliberate wartime effort to demonstrate the U.S. in action on the screen. The government ordered that diverse Americans be positively portrayed to boost the U.S. image worldwide.

There is hope, of course. In 1983 Gregory Nava directed the successful independent film, *El Norte*, the compelling saga of a brother and sister who made their way from Guatemala to the United States for the chance to work, and the many obstacles they faced on their journey. Nava went on to direct *Selena*, the enormously successful movie about a young Latina singer whose career was cut short when she was shot to death by the former president of her fan club.

Those successes prompted New Line Cinema to sign Nava to develop several Latino-themed films with crossover appeal, the first deal of its kind to recognize the second-largest group of ticket buyers in the U.S. The deal has been described as one that allows Nava to develop as many as eight projects — some of which will be handled by younger, lesser-known directors. Although most of the films will likely be budgeted at about $10 million, considerably lower than the $53 million average studio project, it offers Nava the chance to show Latino films can be mainstream successes as well, and not simply niche-market productions.

There have been other positive examples of minority success in the entertainment industry. One of the most important was *The Bill Cosby Show*, whose story was not about being black, but about being a family, with two professional parents trying to raise their children to be contributing members of society. Cosby managed to demonstrate what was possible for minorities in television. That a Hispanic has not yet rivaled Cosby's success may only be a matter of vision – or lack of it — on the part of the producers, writers, directors, actors, and studio management.

There is no question that the Hispanic community has its share of Dr. Heathcliff Huxtables, Hispanic families who exemplify the central values of their culture family loyalty, religious faith, a strong work ethic, and the will and determination to succeed. How much the establishment that rules the entertainment industry is willing to portray these families onscreen remains to be seen.

"Progress, where it exists, is rarely continuous," Woll concluded. "If there's a lesson in this continuing pattern, it may be that film stereotypes are a convenient shorthand for ideas moviemakers expect viewers to hold. Perhaps only if we change our ideas and broaden our concepts can we prevent the repetition of this century of stereotype."

Community Advocacy
Raul Yzaguirre

As the president and chief executive officer of the National Council of La Raza (NCLR), one of the largest Hispanic nonprofit and nonpartisan organizations in the U.S., Raul Yzaguirre has championed the betterment of the Hispanic-American community. For his leadership and commitment to community activism, Yzaguirre received the Order of the Aztec Eagle, the highest honor given by the government of Mexico in 1993. He was the first Hispanic to receive a Rockefeller Public Service Award for Outstanding Public Service from Princeton University (1979), and served as a Fellow for the Harvard University Institute of Politics at the John F. Kennedy School of Government, and on the executive committee of the Leadership Conference on Civil Rights.

CHAPTER EIGHT

A Call to Action

There is a long and prolonged bugle call that's been ringing in the ears of America for as long as Hispanics can remember, a call no one wants to answer, a summoning few want to acknowledge. Is anyone listening?

It does not call us to defend our freedom, our allies, or foreign soil. It is not a call to take arms against enemies. This is a call, America, to embrace and lift a people who are your own, who toil and live and dream alongside other Americans – Americans who happen to be Hispanic. It is time to answer the call.

The story of Latinos in America is not so difficult to understand. It is not unlike any other immigrant account in American history – except that this is the original immigrant story that had its beginnings more than 500 years ago. And it is a story that today continues to evolve *right before our eyes.*

The story of Latinos in America is rich with cultural pageantry, family values, religious faith, a proud language, unshakable loyalties – all strong virtues flourishing in a country built on strength and virtue. It is the story of people who fully embrace the concepts and ideals of Americanism – hard work, unbridled determination, and a spirit to be free and to believe that anything is possible.

The story is moving toward a state of urgency as Hispanics grapple with monumental social challenges that extend far beyond their communities, and which could have far-reaching ramifications on the future of the United States. There are pressing issues at the doorstep of America, yet the door remains tightly shut.

This is not a story about handouts, nor is it about presumptuous birthrights or self-endowed privileges. It is a classic American story about a group of people who have been patient, hopeful, and respectful, but who also have been made to feel neglected, excluded, and frustrated. In the past, we were not as explicit as we should have been about what happened to us or what we *wanted* to happen to us. We have been respectfully quiet. We rarely raised our voices. But that, too, may change *right before our eyes.*

Where Is the Leadership?

For years, Hispanics have listened to overtures from politicians and public officials who patronize them every two years, every four years, or whenever an election is at hand and votes are needed. Promises are made, hands shaken, babies kissed. One day Hispanic voters are political darlings; the next day, stale bread. They wait for the promises, and the promises never come.

And they call Latinos the people of *mañana?*

The 2004 election year is no different. Presidential candidates have trotted out their Spanish-language television ads, hoping to ingratiate themselves to as many as 7 to 8 million voters who could very well affect the political outcome in 22 states, six critically. In past elections, Latinos have voted, on average, at a ratio of 2:1 in favor of Democratic candidates. This year the polls show that as many as 20 percent of Latino voters in some key states are undecided.

So it is not surprising that the presidential candidates are in front of Latino audiences. The Democratic presidential hopeful Senator John Kerry, after praising "Hispanics contributions to our country," ended one speech with the well-recognized Cesar Chavez chant, *"¡Si se puede!"* (Yes, we can!). President

George W. Bush, who is adept at utilizing Spanish phrases he picked up in Texas, unleashed caustic Spanish-language ads attacking Kerry.

But when the last piece of confetti has hit the floor on election night, it will be interesting to see what handful of Hispanic nominees will be considered for posts in the executive branch. Will those posts be on the softer side of government, like the Department of Health and Human Services, the Department of Housing and Urban Development, or one of those sub-cabinet posts, like the head of the Small Business Administration? Will it be too much to expect a Hispanic to land a top-level Cabinet job?

The images of Secretary of State Colin L. Powell and National Security Advisor Condoleezza Rice, two prominent, skilled officials who happen to be black, handling issues of national importance and representing America before world leaders, will surely stay in the minds of a generation of impressionable black youth, who will dream – realistically – that they might one day ascend to the highest office in the land.

And who can blame them? Aside from Powell and Rice, there are a host of other black role models in the highest echelons of both the public and private sector. Blacks are represented on the U.S. Supreme Court with Clarence Thomas, and in top-level Cabinet posts. If the polls are right, there will be a black senator from Illinois, the first since Sen. Carol Moseley-Braun, who served from 1993-1999, and later became ambassador to New Zealand. In 1991, Ruth J. Simmons was named president of Brown University, making her the first black president of an Ivy League school.

In the private sector, there are many role models, blacks who are running major organizations – Richard Parsons, CEO at AOL Time Warner, the world's largest media company; Stan O'Neal, chairman of the board, chief executive officer and president at Merrill Lynch, one of the world's leading financial services providers with more than 48,000 employees worldwide; Ken Chenault, chairman and CEO at American Express, which generated more than $25 billion in revenues in 2003; and Frank Raines, CEO of Fannie Mae, the country's second largest corporation in terms of assets and the nation's largest source of financing for home mortgages with 5,055 employees.

Each of these individuals creates a powerful image. The decisions they make affect thousands of people, including those of their own race. These individuals confirm the notion that viable change starts at the top, and unless you are navigating at those levels, unless you are operating inside a corporate boardroom as an active voting member, unless you're in the driver's seat as either a chairman, CEO, or COO, change will very likely not happen. Not as long as you are on the outside looking in.

With all due respect to our black brethren, this book is not about Hispanics ascending at their expense. It is not about blacks losing ground while Hispanics inch forward. This is not a skirmish between blacks and Hispanics.

What Hispanics do wonder, though, is why, when white Americans speak about the Civil Rights Movement, it's only in reference to African Americans? Hispanics suffered through their share of racial segregation (housing, schools, churches, movie theaters, water fountains, jails, graveyards). In Texas, in the 1950s and 60s, if a Latino child got caught speaking Spanish on the playground or in the classroom, the youth was marched straight to the principal's office and paddled.

Hispanics also wonder why, when corporate America speaks of minority hiring, it is only in terms of hiring black employees? Or why discussions about diversity seem to be cast in terms of black head counts.

Hispanics would love to engage in shared destiny – not just with other ethnic minorities, but a shared destiny with mainstream America. A shared destiny where there are level playing fields, from the playgrounds to the corporate boardrooms. A shared destiny where Hispanics don't have to overcompensate to be accepted. A shared destiny that allows Hispanics to share in the American dream without caveats, qualifiers, or extenuating circumstances.

Can it happen? Of course it can. The black community has already blazed the trail. They have shown the way. Hispanics are no less capable.

Is it not time for Hispanics to cut their own path to the halls of power, in both the public and private sector? It is incomprehensible that Latinos, having lived and worked in North America for more than 500 years, have been excluded from the decision-making levels.

Somewhere a bright-eyed, Latino youth with a genius IQ and a heart full of hope is asking his parents, "Mom, Dad, has there ever been a Hispanic presidential candidate?"

"No."

"A vice presidential candidate?"

"No, not unless you count Peter Camejo, who was named by independent presidential candidate Ralph Nader as his running mate in this year's election – and what do you think the chances of that pair getting elected are?"

"What about a senator?"

"Two, but none since 1977."

"Justices on the U.S. Supreme Court?"

"Never."

"A speaker of the U.S. House of Representatives?"

"No."

"President of the U.S. Senate? A majority leader or minority leader of the senate?"

"No."

"Secretary of state?"

"No."

"Is there a Fortune 100 CEO?"

"No."

"Any presidents of a top 10 university?"

"No."

"What about the head of a major scientific research organization?"

"No."

"Head of a top 10 advertising agency?"

"No."

Does anyone doubt that talented Hispanic youths might have trouble finding national figures who can serve as role models?

According to New America Alliance (NAA), collectively, the 73 Fortune

1000 companies classified as commercial banks, securities firms, and savings institutions have 936 director seats and 793 executive positions. U.S. Latinos hold 28 board seats, or about 3 percent, and only 20 executive positions, or 2.5 percent. Of the 10,314 director positions on the boards of the nation's Fortune 1000 companies, Latinos occupy only 202 seats, less than 2 percent overall, according to the NAA.

Where is the leadership? How can you lead when you're not allowed to participate?

For years, people have talked about the so-called "glass ceiling" that ethnic minorities and women have had to break through. Based on the statistics, Hispanics seem to be banging their heads on a concrete ceiling. It's difficult to dream about reaching for the stars when you can't even see them.

And this at a time when countless press stories are trumpeting Hispanics as the largest and fastest growing minority group in the United States. At a time when corporate America is content to cart away much of the $700 billion that Latinos are generating in purchasing power. Companies certainly are changing their marketing techniques, but in the grander scheme of things, they are not changing the way they do business with Hispanics. Latino dollars are flowing in, but Hispanics continue to be excluded from corporate boardrooms and from senior level posts.

Where is the accountability? How can the elements of inclusion be successfully implemented?

Latino workers represent one out of every eight workers in the American workforce. By 2020, that number will increase to one in six, and by mid-century, one out of every four workers will be Hispanic, according to projections from the U.S. Bureau of Labor and Statistics. It is not enough for corporate officers to boast that 20 to 30 percent of their workforce is Hispanic when there is negligible representation at the middle and executive levels. That is not diversity.

Unless there are plans to find, groom, and nurture Hispanic leadership within the corporate ranks, what are the rank and file to think? That the only people capable of leading them are non-Hispanics? That, too, is not diversity.

While many Hispanic leaders recognize that the immense economic spending power of the Latino community represents a form of financial influence that has never been used, there are also those who believe that this power means little unless it is harnessed and leveraged. Which begs the question, what are Hispanic organizations prepared to do to effect change? How far are they prepared to take it?

The movie spoof, *A Day Without a Mexican*, was recently released in California. The plot was predicated on the idea of the state's entire Latino workforce staying home for one day. The result is statewide economic chaos, with employers having to perform tasks nobody else wants to do.

One long-time Latino demographer mused, tongue-in-cheek, that if terrorists really wanted to bring the United States to its knees, they should convince Hispanics to not work for two weeks. No janitors. No dishwashers. No daycare providers. No landscapers. No restaurant waiters. No doctors or nurses. No construction laborers. No fruit and vegetable farm workers. No teachers. No cooks. No Mexican food. No attorneys. No home cleaning services. No architects. No child care. No meat packers. No hospital and court interpreters. No mechanics. No secretaries.

Hispanics are getting all of this attention, all the while wondering what their votes and hard work can earn them. They wonder what their tax dollars truly buy when they see schools that are dilapidated and poorly equipped, that are understaffed and administered by board members who have lost touch with the communities they are supposed to serve.

And yet there are policy pundits claiming America cannot survive in a global economy when half of all Hispanic children are not graduating from high school, which, by the way, is not true. It's bad enough that dropout rates are a miserable 20 to 25 percent without the critics piling on. Lest they forget, someone should tell them it's difficult to fall out of the basement window.

So what has this working-class ethic earned Hispanics? Despite that they are the most proportionally employed group in the country, more than one in three are without medical insurance. Their personal physicians are residents in hospital emergency rooms or overworked doctors at free public clinics.

Accidental deaths on the job are the third-leading cause of death (primarily in the construction industry) among all Latinos, according to statistics from the Centers for Disease Control and Prevention.

Hispanic leadership is starting to see what demographers have seen for years – critical mass is taking shape. The Hispanic population train is barreling down the track at incredible speed. The potential for economic and political currency is enormous. Forty million people today, 100 million by the midpoint of the 21st century, fully one quarter of all Americans, according to U.S. census projections. Some demographers insist the numbers are low-ball projections because they exclude undocumented immigrants. They predict the number of Latinos in 2050 could actually go as high as 150 million – approaching 40 percent of all Americans.

The question has been asked, "How much will Hispanics change America, and how much will America change them?" It is a question social scientists will mull for years to come. But whether it's 100 million or 150 million, changes are inevitable. It is not a matter of if, but when. And Hispanics are pressing forward and boldly asking, "Why not today?"

Voting Power

It will be 20 years this November since Cesar Chavez, the late farm labor activist and founder of the United Farm Workers Union of America, addressed the Commonwealth Club of California in San Francisco. In perhaps his most memorable speech, Chavez recounted for the attendees how the UFW had kept its resolve, refusing to flinch in the face of intense grower opposition.

Chavez noted how, by using computers, direct mail, and advertising techniques, the UFW had been more successful during the first 11 months of a boycott in 1984 than the union had been in the previous 14 years. Chavez said, "The other trend that gives us hope is the monumental growth of Hispanic influence in this country and what that means in increased population, increased social and economic clout, and increased political influence."

Chavez noted that in 1984 there were hundreds of thousands of registered

Latino voters in California, 85 percent Democrat, 13 percent Republican. In 1975 there were only 200 Hispanic elected officials in California. In 1984, he said, there were more than 400 elected judges, city council members, mayors, and legislators.

"Like the other immigrant groups, the day will come when we win our economic and political rewards, which are in keeping with our numbers in society," Chavez said. "The day will come when the politicians do the right things by our people out of political necessity and not out of charity or idealism."

Chavez would be happy to know that nationwide there are now more than 6,000 Latinos who have either been elected or appointed to official positions, a long way from the 400 California public officials of 1984.

In this presidential election year, Chavez's prophetic words are part inspirational, part haunting, and have as much currency now as they did two decades ago. Hispanic leaders are bracing themselves like never before. Unprecedented media attention is focused on the Latino community. As the largest and fastest growing ethnic group in the country, there is talk that voter registration drives could scoop up 7 to 8 million eligible voters by November.

Plainly put, it's time to put up or shut up. And that goes for voters and politicians alike. In baseball jargon, you can't hit if you don't swing. It is not enough to complain about how lousy things are. In fact, unless you cast your vote, you really don't have the genuine right to complain.

Be honest: Have you registered? If not, why not? More important, when will you register? If you're a legal resident, have you applied to become a citizen? How can we elect our candidate of choice if we don't vote? How can we throw out that unresponsive bum who's living out of the public till unless we vote? Hardly anything we do as American citizens means more than casting our vote.

For the record, Hispanics pulled up the statistical rear during the 2000 presidential election. Of the total number of Hispanic citizens who were eligible to vote, only 45.1 percent, or about 6 million, went into the voting booth, versus 61.8 percent and 56.9 percent for whites and blacks, respectively. That means more than half – approximately 7.2 million Hispanics – chose to sit that election out, chose to not exercise their rights as Americans citizens. What's the point of working so hard and paying those city, state, and federal taxes? What's the point of wanting a better life for the children, of demanding a place in American society, unless we participate by registering to vote and then actually voting?

The Hispanic voter results in 2000 and 1996 represent the two lowest voter turnouts (as a percentage of eligible voters) during the last 20 years. Some might argue that 45 percent of a large number is still significant, and that 6 million votes should not be denigrated — and it would true. But when white citizens outpoll Hispanics by almost 17 percentage points and black citizens by almost 12 points, some may legitimately question the Latino community's level of commitment. Imagine this: 12 percentage points would have meant an additional 1.6 million votes in 2000; an additional 17 points would have brought in 2.26 million votes. That's political capital that cannot be squandered.

For example, in 2024, the U.S. Hispanic population is projected to be about 65 million, according to the census. Replicate the statistical results of the 2000 presidential election in 2024, and 45.1 percent turns into almost 11 million votes. A big number indeed. But it would also mean 13.2 million stayed home. An even bigger number. What good is it to be the largest and fastest growing ethnic group in America if political capital of that magnitude is wasted?

Probably at no time in election history has the Hispanic vote been as critical as it is this year for both President Bush and the Democratic Party's John Kerry. Political strategists in both camps are furiously mapping out plans that, they believe, will lure Hispanic votes one way or the other. The political maneuvering will be crucial to both candidates as key states are going to be in play, including Arizona, Oregon, Nevada, Colorado, and New Mexico.

Raul Yzaguirre, national director of National Council of La Raza, the country's largest national constituency-based Hispanic organization, said his organization wants to send a message to the candidates — that the Latino electorate will be a force in the 2004 elections, and the past treatment of the Latino community won't be tolerated come November.

"We are afraid that we will see a continuation of a pattern, particularly in 2000, where there was a lot of emphasis on style, marketing, and speaking a few phrases in Spanish and identifying with a particular star or celebrity in our community," said Yzaguirre. "What we are demanding and insisting is that this needs to be more about substance than style."

Yzaguirre said neither party should take anything for granted regarding Hispanic votes. NCLR polls have already determined that while there is still deep interest in key issues, such as immigration, the Latino community is just as concerned about education, jobs, the economy, health concerns, discrimination, and civil rights issues.

The focus will be on accountability and results, Yzaguirre said. "At the end of the day, the strength of the Latino voice in leveraging policy change is measured in the results that affect individuals' lives in the community itself."

Purchasing Power

With billions of Latino dollars being rung up at store registers this year, perhaps consumers should consider treating stores with the same scrutiny and demand for accountability voters use on politicians. In straight economic terms, $700 billion does represent economic purchasing power. Is there an opportunity to leverage that power for the greater good of a community?

Should consumers and consumer groups devise a means to metrically identify and grade stores and their parent companies that have, for example, exemplary outreach programs in a Latino community? Should good corporate enterprises be cited favorably for their hiring practices, their customer service, for providing bilingual capabilities, for supporting local civic causes and youth sports teams? How about participation in local foundations that help the needy, the sick, the impaired, the elderly? Have they formed civic partnerships with local school systems?

On the flip side, what about a metric system that penalizes and demands accountability of stores and parent companies that do not perform up to prescribed standards?

Why not an annual report card that bestows "favored" status on the best corporate citizens – a mini-version of the national Malcolm Baldrige Awards? The Baldrige Award is given by the president to businesses — manufacturing and service, small and large — and to education and health care organizations that are determined as outstanding in seven areas: leadership, strategic planning, customer and market focus, information and analysis, human resource focus, process management, and business results.

This Hispanic report card could measure the appointment of Latinos to corporate boards, or gauge companies based on the hires of Hispanics in top-level positions. Let's not forget corporate vendors, or contracts awarded to Hispanic businesses, which are growing at four times the rate of any other small business group, according to the U.S. Hispanic Chamber of Commerce.

Hispanic community groups could create a national forum to discuss the key elements of the report card, and disseminate the results to other Hispanic organizations via newspapers, radio, television, magazines, and electronic messages. They would ask Hispanics to take action on non-performing companies by not patronizing them and, at the same time, promote those companies that do.

Are there other things that could make the relationship between Hispanic retailers and consumers a busier two-way street? Are there opportunities to foster economic development with local Hispanic businesses? The cash registers are already ringing. Can Hispanics leverage this purchasing power into political and economic strength?

No one professes to have all the answers, or even the best answers. The intent of this book was to freeze frame – as best as one can with such a galloping story – the state of Hispanics in America, and assess their impact on the American economic, business, social, and political landscape. The motivation, too, was to provoke thought and discussion about critical policy issues. Ultimately it was to invoke – yet again — a call to action for the concerns of Hispanics and America.

By design, there are no moral issues at stake here. There are no false pretenses. Hispanic leaders have espoused the need for time, care, attention, funding, and commitment for every issue covered in this book. Many people said the same things 20 to 30 years ago. Is it any wonder that some of them grew weary and despondent? Even a bit jaded?

So we, too, wade in with our own words, our own recommendations, and with the notion that the ideas which follow will add another voice. We believe it's time to raise the decibel level a few notches. Hispanics are productive, contributing members of this society. They proved it before, and they'll have no problem proving it again. This time, however, the American public needs to know Hispanics are dead-on serious about issues of inclusion, accountability, and if necessary, political and economic retribution. To this, we offer the following:

SCORECARDS: Hispanic organizations need to develop comprehensive scorecards to hold accountable both the public and private sectors for, among other things, board representation, executive placement, hiring practices, contracts with Hispanic-owned businesses, and financial support of Hispanic foundations and civic projects.

Local, regional, and national Hispanic organizations need to formulate the scorecard, explain and distribute it to the community, and ultimately mobilize around the results. It will serve notice to company executives, public entities, and public officials who are rewarded for good behavior or cited for poor performance with "favored" versus "non-favored" status.

LEADERSHIP REPRESENTATION: It is time for corporate America to appoint Hispanics to corporate boards in higher numbers, reflecting more representation and a stronger commitment to the Latino marketplace. Further, it is imperative that corporate America appoint Hispanics to the top 10 management posts within company organizations. Companies that make good on these commitments should be given a "favored" designation to reward their efforts. Companies that don't comply would be cited for poor performance, and given a "non-favored" company tag, subject to repercussive measures from the Hispanic community. Similar measures could be outlined for public entities and public officials.

PROCUREMENT CONTRACTS: It is time for corporate America to formulate strong business relationships with Hispanic-owned entrepreneurs, who can serve as either direct suppliers or as subcontractors to suppliers in matters of procurement. The level of contracting would be based on the level of business from the Hispanic community. As with leadership representation above, companies would be measured, graded, and assessed with "favored" or "non-favored" status depending on their participation. There are 2 million Hispanic-owned businesses in the U.S. today; that number is expected to grow to more than 3 million by 2010.

EMPLOYMENT: Corporate America needs to ensure the hiring of Hispanics will result in their placement at all levels of the organization, and that they have a realistic opportunity for advancement. Hiring people is not the issue. Hiring people in the right ways and promoting them is the issue. Organizations cannot claim Hispanic parity if their lower-level employee counts are heavily weighted, while middle- to upper-level ranks are empty. Again, the scorecard will determine a company's final assessment.

CHARITABLE CONTRIBUTIONS: Corporate foundations should assess their level of charitable contributions to the Hispanic community with respect to the level of business the parent company conducts within the community. Funding should be proportionally allocated. This area, too, would be assessed via the scorecard method.

The simplicity of these ideas might leave some people asking for details about the process. Realistically, there are no sets of instructions. The idea of using scorecards is as diverse and creative as the subgroups that make up the Hispanic community. The simplicity of our call to action doesn't require the creation of any new mechanisms other than creating the scorecards, disseminating them to the community, and then acting on the results in a positive or repercussive manner.

Consider the fact that every company has a board of directors. Every company has senior management. Every company has procurement. Every company does employee hiring. Practically every company gets involved in charitable giving. Simplicity works.

The power and strength of the scorecard will be determined by how far each Hispanic community or organization is prepared to go to achieve its goals. The central questions of the exercise are these: What are you prepared to do? How far are you prepared to take it, especially for companies that earn themselves a "non-favored" status?

Cesar Chavez used to say that every time you entered a supermarket and you chose not buy grapes, you cast a vote in favor of the boycott. You could cast your vote as many times as you wanted because the polls never closed. Corporate America and the political community have two primary motivating factors – profits and votes, respectively. Remember, simplicity works. "Favored" companies versus "non-favored" companies. "Favored" politicians versus "non-favored" politicians.

If America is to remain globally competitive, it must engage its energetic and youthful Hispanic community, and convince its members to take a more active role in rectifying the business, economic, social, and political deficiencies that have historically disaffected Latinos. But in order for America to succeed, we must see inclusive leadership among Hispanics at the executive levels of government and corporate America. It can happen. After all, one of the great strengths of this country is its promise of representative government. Inclusiveness is an undeniable standard of that system, and the underpinning of shared destiny.

Hispanics bring with them critical elements that dovetail neatly into America's strategic plans to remain a strong global competitor. Hispanics provide a growing work force that will play an integral part in America's future. Remember, by 2050 one in four workers will be Latinos. Hispanics will continue to fuel the economy through its growing consumer spending power – $1 trillion in five years and growing exponentially as the population numbers rise. The global arena will require multilingual and multicultural skills and approaches. Most Hispanics already live in and navigate those worlds. America can only benefit from those valuable traits.

In the next few years, as the country's Baby Boomer generation slips into retirement, many will wonder if the faltering Social Security system will yield reasonable payouts. If you are a Latino 20 years from now and you're paying into a Social Security system for the same people who excluded you 20 years before, how will you feel? How would you vote? Where would you spend your money?

This is not about threats – it's about human behavior. The ability to embrace the concept of shared destiny, and the idea that issues related to leadership, corporate representation, education, poverty, home ownership, health care, and safety are not just Latino issues – they are American issues that are challenging us now, right before our eyes.

There is a bugle call, an inspiring tune but with an urgent pitch that beckons all Hispanic Americans to come together. For what, you ask? How about curing the ills of poor education, poverty, illness? How about achieving equality under American laws? Do you hear the call? Will you answer it?

There is a call for Hispanic Americans, imploring Latino leadership at all levels to come together, despite country of origin, despite income class, despite race, to set aside political differences, personal agendas and jaded cynicism. There is much to do. It is not about wallowing in self-pity or banking on the rest of America to throw a safety net. It is about taking responsibility. It is about earning respect. It is about unshakable pride. Sweeping changes are coming. Do you hear the call? Will you answer it? Because it is about you, about us, about this great country, the United States of America.